MW00806654

Pumps in the Pulpit is a literary
Angel Wellington. In this book
upon her life as well as the intricacies of pastoral demands and
expectations. She openly and transparently discusses the value of
women in ministry and many of the challenges women face in
a predominantly male leadership institution. You will be greatly
blessed and enlightened through her writings.

—Bishop Charles Ellis III
Pastor of Greater Grace Temple in Detroit, Michigan
Presiding Bishop of Pentecostal Assemblies of the World

Brilliant and unpredictable, *Pumps in the Pulpit* is worth the read!
Without fighting or forcing a fit, Pastor Angel simply shares her
amazing experience, which causes us to reevaluate women, ministry, and the way each impacts the other. The wisdom woven
throughout these pages will make you think…then, rethink
everything you thought you knew about a woman with a Word.

—Dr. Dee Dee Freeman
First Lady of Spirit of Faith Christian Center-
Prince George's Co. and Howard Co., Md.
Founder of God's Glamorous Girls

I thought it befitting to share my sentiment. Pastor Angel has
written a tremendous work for the body of Christ: ministers,
couples, parents, musicians, women, and church members. If
the truth she imparts is received, the kingdom of God will grow
exponentially, while the middle wall of partition stays the way
Jesus left it. As my wife and co-laborer, she has my whole-hearted
admiration and full backing of what she was born to do. "Pumps"
proves that. It is a Spirit-driven ride of ups and downs, ins and
outs, bends and turns. When we finally rest, we know what to
do…all of us, male and female. Thanks for your spiritual sensi-
tivity and perfect timing. I am pumped up!!!

—Antonio E. Wellington
Pastor, Descending Dove Christian Center
Wilmington, North Carolina

PUMPS
in the
PULPIT

Angel A. Wellington

CREATION
HOUSE

PUMPS IN THE PULPIT by Angel Wellington
Published by Creation House
A Charisma Media Company
600 Rinehart Road
Lake Mary, Florida 32746
www.charismamedia.com

Unless otherwise noted, all Scripture quotations are from the New King James Version of the Bible. Copyright © 1979, 1980, 1982 by Thomas Nelson, Inc., publishers. Used by permission.

Library of Congress Cataloging-in-Publication Data: 2014941150
International Standard Book Number: 978-1-62136-766-6
E-book International Standard Book Number: 978-1-62136-767-3

While the author has made every effort to provide accurate telephone numbers and Internet addresses at the time of publication, neither the publisher nor the author assumes any responsibility for errors or for changes that occur after publication.

First edition

14 15 16 17 18— 987654321
Printed in the United States of America

DEDICATION:

This effort is consecrated and dedicated to Christ Jesus, Who extended His punctured hand to escort me into His pulpit!

This space is reserved for:

Dr. Barbara M. Amos

Dr. Audrey F. Bronson

Mo. Lettie Cohen

Dr. Claudette Copeland

Dr. Cynthia Hale

Dr. Millicent Hunter

Dr. Cynthia James

Dr. Jacqueline McCullough

Dr. Vashti McKenzie

Mo. Irene Oakley

Pastor Susie Owens

Bishop E.C. Reems

Bishop Ida B. Robinson

Dr. Carolyn Showell

Bishop Amy B. Stevens

Pastor Rosie Wallace-Brown

Bishop L. C. Williams

And countless others too numerous to name, whose own sacred, sometimes perilous, steps cleared the way for women like me to stand tall in the "shoes" God made to fit our pretty feet!

CONTENTS

PART I: PLACES

PART II: PEOPLE

PART III: THINGS

FOREWORD

MY PERSONAL JOURNEY with Pastor Angel Wellington began many years ago. Even then, as a young and energetic college student, she emoted an unforgettable enthusiasm for the Lord and a passion for His work. Ultimately, her goal has always been to bring persons into the saving knowledge of Jesus Christ and for them to experience a *resurrected life* in Him. Through the years our relationship has grown, matured, and experienced transitions. I would dare to humbly share that I have served as a teacher, pastor, bishop, mentor, spiritual covering, and friend.

This book is a personal account of some of the various experiences and nuances that have shaped and molded the dynamic minister that I have grown to affectionately call Pastor Angel. Her serious upbringing as a youth in the church, under the watchful eye of a praying mother, has been very beneficial in her years of development as a woman. A devoted wife, mother, and pastor, she has been blessed with the leading of the Lord to manage each with style and substance. Additionally, she certainly brings an aura of grace, dignity, and integrity to the pulpit.

Though this writing is indeed an inspiration for women who sense the call of God upon their lives, it is equally inspiring for any person yearning to capture a glimpse of the faithfulness of God at work in the affairs of His people. Although there are unique challenges for females in the body of Christ, Pastor Angel understands and conveys the power of the anointing of the Holy Spirit in the life of every believer, male or female. In myriad ways, she displays overwhelming confidence in her calling from God—a confidence that transcends the need for her pursuits to be gender-driven and/or gender-validated.

Her years in ministry have yielded triumphs and challenges, all of which are the foundation for this writing. Each chapter of this motivational narrative provides insight into various portions of her journey and affords you the opportunity to participate in the dramatic written presentation of an eventful and effective ministry.

Since meeting her, I have never ceased to be amazed at her creativity and versatility. As you read *Pumps in the Pulpit*, be assured that Pastor Angel's unique and vivid writing style mirrors her personality.

For those of you who must operate at times on the fringes, you will definitely be encouraged as you read this book. You will be privy to various facets of her God-inspired life and will find her transparency very refreshing and certainly admirable. A woman of integrity, Pastor Angel does not hesitate to articulate her disappointments and pain. Having walked alongside her on different roads and paths, I have observed some of her lowest moments, as well as prayed with her through difficult times. It is refreshing to know, however, that someone, in this case Pastor Angel, will readily admit that regardless of how mightily they may be used of the Lord, there are times when you almost long for Him to use someone else! Resilient and determined, she has always traveled the path back to the foot of the cross!

For those facing uncertainty, you can be inspired to follow the call of God into unchartered waters as Pastor Angel has repeatedly done with amazing outcomes. Her unique approach to ministry provides interesting reading for those who also find themselves challenged by distinctive situations and circumstances. You will laugh, cry, be encouraged, or perhaps be moved with amazement. Adversity has strengthened her movement toward the fulfillment of a vision that is yet unfolding. Having personally walked through portions of this journey with Pastor Angel, I can say with assurance that her life and journey can be viewed as a wealthy resource for the body of Christ. I am certain that you will not only read this book now, but you may find yourself using it as a future source of reference, since we can all readily identify with so much of its content.

I am always humbled and honored when God, who can use anyone that He chooses, and certainly persons more suitable than me, allows me to participate in some small way in the development of His people. As my spiritual daughter, I am extremely proud of all of Pastor Angel's contributions to the *family* of God. In terms of decorum, I am so proud of the *"beautiful feet"* that are in the *Pumps in the Pulpit*. To God be the glory!

—Dr. Barbara M. Amos
Presiding Prelate:
Faith Deliverance Christian Fellowship
Kinston, North Carolina

Acknowledgments:

Antonio, you know that I love you, you just don't know how much! There is nothing you possess with which to measure. The Lover of our souls keeps stretching the tape.

Sterling, thanks for asking the kinds of questions that require book-length answers. And adding to my joy without effort!

Both of you make me want to be the wife and mother you act like I am.

Descending Dove Christian Center: We were meant to be together. Love that Dove!

Dr. Barbara M. Amos: Thanks for encouraging me to write what left me bleeding and broken, but made me better.

Dr. Katie Davis: I so appreciate you believing that the words God gave me had spirit and life!

Bishop Odell McFarland, Jr.: My most humble gratitude for lending me your ears, while rendering your prayers.

Charisma Media/Creation House: What an honor to have the backing of a brand that has distinguished itself among publishers as a standard of excellence and sustenance. I am humbled and grateful that *you* were my introduction to the world of writing.

Some prudent soul once said that every life needs to be edited. I poured a great deal of my life onto these pages and needed someone to see what I couldn't and change what I wanted to. Elizabeth Wiggers, thanks for "seeing" me through and never seeming to be overwhelmed. I pray our divine connection made *your* "baby leap!"

Berta Coleman: You walked me through a mammoth task and simplified it to its lowest common denominator. Your grace, dignity, and attention to detail almost made me forget that this was my first literary venture. The pleasure has most assuredly been mine!

INTRODUCTION

MY SON POSED the question, "Do you like being a pastor?" I paused, perhaps longer than I should have or ever expected I might. Prior to that point, no one had asked. I hadn't even asked myself. Certainly, the question required an answer, so why was one not readily available? I thought quickly and intensely. While mused, I also considered *not* discouraging any call God may have for our son's life or making him feel sad, mad, or bad for me or our family. *Where were words when I needed them?* Apparently not near my tongue, but scurrying about my head trying to organize. What sounded like one finally escaped: "Um?" I muttered, and then repeated his query for borrowed time. I said *something* that day. I do not recall what. I have not actually answered...until now.

Allow me to explain my dilemma. I absolutely love the people to whom I'm sent. But that wasn't the question. This wasn't about them, but the position, the place, and even the pressure it can entail. The births, deaths, graduations, celebrations, recitals, parties, games, court cases, meetings, dinners, sessions, house blessings, weddings, situations, family feuds, hospital visits, after midnight calls, on-call posturing, planning, praying, presiding, and preaching are no small tasks. In addition to instructions in Christianity, I have been inclined to teach how to clean house, study, drive, create and live by a budget, wrap gifts, vote, write, shop and save, dress for success, socialize, interview, parent, and make marriage work. Changing diapers, tires, and car oil are, too, on my clergy list of things to impart. *Anything* pertaining to life and godliness is subject to full disclosure in my attempt to equip His body. This is no mere job or career. Nor is it a position to be trifled with. Answering this "call" commands one's life.

I recall a special education teacher once sharing that she wouldn't be in school for a while because she was scheduled to "take her time." I inquired further, unsure of her reference. I learned that day that special education teachers, at least at our school, were strongly urged to take a certain amount of time off due to the nature of their job. She suggested that issues associated with the special needs student were often so great that they had the propensity to negatively affect the teacher's personal life. So to avoid "burn-out" or over-exertion, they took mandatory respites to regroup.

Though that information was given to me many years ago, I have often reflected on the wisdom of that system. The operative words in her statement were time off. As a pastor, I have, thankfully, been granted breaks, vacations, and Sabbaths; but being "off" is the rest we must *labor to enter into*. We are always "on" and have to practice, repeatedly, the art of pulling aside and the act of letting go.

In addition to the aforementioned, a pastor has the charge of conveying Biblical truths, living Christianity "out-loud," taking people to Heaven, and finishing "the race" well. Being a pastor was not my idea, invention, or inspiration. I did not aspire to it or ascribe to it. I had not entertained the thought, notion, or possibility. There was no indication that I would be or inclination to try. I simply said yes to the *only* One who asked me. And the rest—is *our* history, outlined in these pages. What I write, I write to our son, his son, and sons and daughters to come; that they may know the way we took and why. Do not despise it, dishonor it or disregard it: it is *how* we got where we are, and we will not pass this way again.

CHAPTER 1
"Let The Church Say . . . A Man!"

THE PASTORS OF my youth were vastly different from those of today. They were not celebrities, socialites, or movie stars. Whether that is right, wrong, or indifferent is not for this discussion; I am simply noting the contrast. The ones I knew, whose tables I ate at, whose children I associated with, and whose work I helped do, were, for the most part, men of distinction. They wore plain suits, drove immaculate vehicles, liked their water glasses filled beside the big pulpit chair, showed-up after service was "hot" (at the end of praise and worship) and "whooped" (preached and sang at the same time). As I remember, they were rarely young, usually rigid, reverent, and always religious. We respected them greatly. What they almost never were was *female*.

It was not that they didn't like women (a few, too much), they just sincerely believed God could not use *a girl* in the same capacity the good ole boys had been called. Those pastors must have, at least, appreciated the feminine factor because women were ever-present. They made-up the majority of all congregations, gave the most in tithe and offering, contributed to *every* phase of *each* building fund, taught all members from Vacation Bible School through Sunday School, planned the programs, made the meals, cleaned and cared for the church, kept the books, showed-up for any service, meeting, or rehearsal, and purposefully made the pastor "look good."

The women of any ministry I have attended emceed, sang, prayed, ushered, announced, directed, fasted, read, typed, sewed, sowed, nursed, drove, counseled, and often prepared, proofread, and practiced the sermons with the pastor. But to mount the pulpit and stand behind the podium to actually preach was "out of order." The idea of her shepherding, though she usually cared for the sheep, was unfathomable. In contradiction, sometimes women would be permitted to "hold down" (pastor for a short period of time) a church until the members could choose a male pastor.

Shamefully, I, too, succumbed to similar thoughts, beliefs, and practices. In my opinion, women could be used in just about any way, with the exception of preacher or pastor. I'm not sure I expanded my slant outside the church because this was my world. Here, she was not welcomed to lead, though she had birthed, nurtured, trained, cared for, and led all her children—sons and daughters—like...a shepherd.

I picked up a small pamphlet one day, thumbing through it while awaiting an appointment. The first thing that struck me was an article about a shepherd *girl*! How embarrassed I was to learn, at this stage of my life, that there were shepherdesses. My "not knowing" spoke more to my prejudice than ignorance. It was not a thought I cared to consider. With the good fruit of my spiritual upbringing was also a full grown weed of rejection. That weed would wrap around the view I had of myself and attempt to strangle any seed of what I, or anyone like me, could do.

When any woman, member, or guest "crossed the line" from presenting to preaching, we referred to that as "boot-legging," making sure she was within earshot of our jest. Though relayed in comedic form, the severity of such an offense could be felt and might just keep the offender from a second invitation. She may have to return to the Sunday school class.

Though many of us knew that the practice of even subtle sexism had to be strange, at best, no one dared divulge their question, "Why?" Why would God not trust them, like them, or use them in the way He would men? Above all, why would He equip them with qualities, individualities, abilities, and skills needed to do the work of ministry; but deny them the place to do so?

I can even recollect some preachers back then suggesting that a woman's menstrual cycle or childbearing served as sufficient proof that she could not "be ready in season *and* out of season." She must not be made to fulfill this call, they insisted. "You can't stop preaching to bleed or give birth. That's how you know God meant this for men!" Surely this was not the strongest or most sensible argument that could be made?

When I learned that the often misrepresented, "women keep silent in the churches" spoke to a particular disorder, I questioned our position on the subject of women in ministry. Many of our own men would have been guilty of violating such laws, since women were seldom silent in our assemblies, except when it was time to render the morning message or teach Bible study. When I discovered that the usually misquoted "man is the head of a woman" was about *a* husband, not *all* men, covering, not controlling, his own wife, I had more questions than substantive answers.

Since there were no real questions ever asked on this subject, there were no pure answers provided; all were tainted, subjective. Most often, men facilitated the discussion and determined the outcome. So back then, we relegated her activities to the following: One Hundred Women in White, women's conferences, one day at convocation, and women's choir on Mother's Day. We'd acknowledge her, inscribe her name on pew plagues, or hang her picture in the vestibule. We'd give her flowers while she lived and hope she'd be placated. Perhaps women would never notice that they were welcomed to stand everywhere in the sanctuary except the "front porch." That platform wasn't big enough for everyone. Later in our ministry, someone had a change of heart, so sisters were allowed to preach, they just could never *pastor* like the brothers. That cherished spot was still reserved for those who "wore the pants," not pumps.

One of the wisest women I love has taught me that "practice doesn't make perfect, it just makes permanent." You can practice *anything* so long that you believe the practice itself is sacred. Subjugating our grandmothers, mothers, sisters, aunts, nieces, and wives cannot be sacred; but it was acceptable, and that made it sanctified in our eyes.

Earlier this week, my morning devotional landed me on the pages of an apropos passage in Scripture, though I recall few messages regarding it. In Numbers 22, the daughters of a man named Zelophehad have been granted an audience with Moses, the priest, other leaders, and the congregation of Israel. The preceding chapters convey the distribution of the promise land and inheritances. Concerning that, these ladies make the case that their father had no sons, so that there was no descendant of his to inherit his portion. No one was left to get his part but them. Since they were women, they had not even been considered. They were appealing to the "powers that be" to include them.

I was enlightened and enlarged by what followed their request. Verse five reveals that Moses, the shepherd who had led this flock and seen God face to face, was not so presumptuous as to conclude that the answer was one he readily knew. So, he "brought their cause before the Lord."

The Lord's reply, they "speak right" proved that Moses had missed something, overlooked something, or forgotten something. But he had gone to the Source, so now he knew what to do. Perhaps our response would be different if we did the same. Perhaps that is why we don't, choosing, rather, to listen to the same voices, read the same literature, attend the same luncheons, vote the same way—too comfortable to relinquish "the big chair." Men I knew, who normally practiced good manners, refused to do so in this respect.

Armed with new information, Moses returned to the congregation and righted the wrong. Not only were they to inherit, but a new *law* was introduced *by God* to make sure no such gender oversight would ever happen, again. A law which ensured that the Old Testament sisters would receive "an inheritance among their father's brethren." I wonder what that same God would say about *His daughters* under the New Covenant of grace.

Not too long ago, I saw one of the pastors I knew as a child on television. How timely! He was all shined-up, still rigid, and religious. As the camera swept over the sanctuary, I saw something else: women I had known and forgotten about. There they sat, *or stood,* supporting *him.* These were women who, once, had something to say—women who advised me, blessed me, developed me and *led* me. But that day they were silent. There was something sad about it. I wondered if they were truly happy, if their joy was ever full? I pondered my own plight and how different my life would be if I just sat saying..."A Man!"

She stepped, surreptitiously. The road beneath her feet was worn and riddled with potential religious sympathizers. As far as she knew, they were rounding up anyone who followed the recently executed. She was one of them, from as far back as his small village. Now in the big city, she was weary, and he was gone. Days of what should have been celebration and commemoration slid into nights of restlessness. Darkness enveloping her and threats invading her were no match for the will to properly lay him down.

When she, finally, arrived at the place, something was skewed. She and her sister friends had been careful to mark the spot and observed the rushed attempt to honor the body of their friend. But in the predawn hours of this first day of the week, the boulder that blocked the entrance before was not where it belonged. If some grave robbers had desiccated this sacred site, removing the dearly departed, she should seek help immediately! And so she ran.

Her "brothers" were close enough to accompany her back to the tomb. The youngest ran quickly, choosing to peek in first. Believing her explanation that the body had been removed, he saw the emptiness for himself. The elder found her report and his response hard to process, requiring closer scrutiny. He went in.

The only things remaining in the cavernous enclosure were the cloths that once shrouded the body of the deceased, lying as if he had just stepped out of them. Away from them was the square fabric used to cover his face. It was neat, folded, as one would a dinner napkin to signal the waiter that he was only away, temporarily. But even signs can be misconstrued when one is mourning. The young man had to see for himself, so he stepped inside. Because no one knew, exactly, what was inferred by the "I will raise it up" statements, every one believed the worst. Two of them left the graveyard to return to grief, and now, bewilderment.

She stayed.

Weeping without, she decided to look, again, hoping she was wrong, thinking she may have missed something. Second takes can make a world of difference. Had she run away, she would have missed her "calling." There they sat: two angels with a burial garment between them. They asked a single question, "Why are you crying?" and were done. Because she did not look

before weeping, nothing inside her was leaping at the possibility.
So, she just stood. But a "bad" stand is better than a "good" run.
The presumed gardener walked up behind the distraught
woman. He echoed the inquiry of the two, with a notable
exception; "Who are you looking for?" She answered the angels:
"I am crying over the body..." She answered the man: "I am
looking for him." Well, there is no need to continue crying...or
looking, for that matter. Jesus called Mary by name, then called
her to carry the good news of His death, burial, and resurrection.

Sharing the Gospel *is* preaching. The Lord, then, ordained the
first female minister. I'm so glad she wasn't the last. I, too, am a
woman. And like the one created from Adam's side, the blood and
water flowing from the second Adam gave new life to me, too (every
birth has blood and water). What the curse of Genesis brought, the
death of Jesus removed. His *and her* dominion was restored. The
stigma and shame were swallowed up by the vicarious death of
Christ. To believe or *behave* any other way is to reject and refuse
God's original plan, reinstated at the cross for anyone who missed
it the first time. Amen!

> "God said, Let us make man in our image, after our likeness...let
> **them** have dominion...male and female created He **them**...God
> blessed **them**..."
>   —GENESIS 1:26–28, Emphasis Added

CHAPTER 2

Prayer Meeting

After working all day, then traveling for hours, we were relieved to see the city limits sign. The trip had been pleasant, though a weight rested on us at any thought of our assignment. To mask the task, we listened to music, told stories, and drank too much juice. We would have eaten, but the situation required consecration, so we fasted, as requested, feasting on fluids. Following the bishop's van were bands of intercessors, prayer warriors who had been in their share of spiritual warfare, and whom I had seen "return with the spoils" time and time again.

We were in our own new van, purchased days before and shining like new money. I was pleased to have it and hoped that the empty seats beside and behind our son's would one day carry his siblings. This trip would put the first miles on the odometer, but far from the last.

The Sunday prior to this Thursday evening was one for the records in the history of Faith Deliverance Christian Center, our church in Norfolk, Virginia. We always had phenomenal worship, thanks, in part, to our pastor who had taught and practiced pure praise and the minister of music who made-up in exhortation what she lacked in size. This dynamic duo led us where they had been, *showing* the congregation how to thank God to our praise place, worship till the glory came, then bask in that glory. Small in stature, these two demonstrated that there was no limit to the dimensions the glory could carry you.

We were "carried" that Sunday to the extent that our pastor could not minister. We made it beyond the veil. With hands extending, knees bending, and tears flowing, a sweet, still presence, lingered. So did we—just sitting, standing or lying. Where could anyone of us go that was equal to, or better than, this? Time must have moved, but we would not, dare not, because we didn't want to break the flow or make our Guest feel that He had worn-out His welcome. So we waited.

Awhile later, the pastor instructed anyone who had to leave to do so in quiet. A brief blessing was pronounced and a few members exited. As things began to "go back to normal," and prior to dismissal, words were heard in the speaker behind me. They were the kind no congregant is comfortable hearing…"I wish to see the Wellingtons in my office before they leave, please."

While the masses made their way to the doors, we went in the direction of the administrative offices. When inside, we were greeted graciously and invited to sit until the pastor was free to speak. We whispered the same concern, "What had we done?" and "Why couldn't we remember?" The wait can best be described as that associated with being called to the principal's office and needing to come-up with an explanation for your recent violation. I knew a little about that, but since no immediate infraction came to mind, I stared at the many pictures of our pastor's exploits.

The door opening startled me. She came to where we were and pulled up a chair. She was, now, dry and changed into fresh clothes. Her face was steady, stern, and serious. She spoke softly and straight to the point. Almost always, her normal approach would include some light banter or quick anecdote, but something was on her heart. "I need you to accompany me this Thursday," she started. "I have just left a meeting with a board of bishops, and we have a situation!"

I refuse to repeat her next words because the security of the innocent and ignorant warrants my confidentiality. What I *will* say is that the situation was dire, pernicious, and volatile. Though fixed on remaining silent, I would soon learn that rumors were spreading far and wide, and that the church had lost favor within the community. Broken pieces would have to be picked up and shattered lives mended years after the fact. So "bleeding" was inevitable.

Our pastor continued, "I am taking a group to the city just to meet with any remaining members of that ministry and pray. If you are available, I'd like for you to go." Already "pricked" by the particulars of her sharing, we looked at each other, and then agreed. Before accepting our answer, she added that the place was in North Carolina, in a small town that few have ever heard of. When she named the place, we laughed because we were among the few who had. One of my older sisters, who lived in North Carolina, had introduced our youngest sister to a gentleman from that area. They married and lived not too far from where we were going to meet. This was getting interesting.

Want to know something even more interesting? Once, while going to visit my sister and her family, we stopped in that same town. Waiting for them to lead us to their place, we got out of the car, ate ice cream from the local Hardees, and took our tiny nephew to throw balls in its play land. It was hot! My sweaty mother, squinting sister, future spouse, and I sat eating melting cream and checking out the place. That didn't' take long. We were on the main road leading in and out, so all the "happenings" were observable from right where we sat.

Born in New York, but reared in a small city myself, this was even different for me. I had a Green Acres moment, playing the theme song in my head and envisioning Park Avenue from some penthouse window. I have relatives who live in rural areas, class-mates who stay in "the country," and friends who get frustrated with anything "city;" but this was just not for me. Not only did I think it, I said it out loud: "I would never be in a place like this!" My sage mama raised her head, adorned her prophetic mantle, then spoke softly, "Baby, never say never! Life is too unpredictable for that."

For the moment, I felt safe within the walls of our pastor's office. Sitting across from her, I imagined how difficult it must be for a prelate. If preaching and teaching were the only things a pastor had to do, it would suffice. But being the presiding officer of states meant overseeing the affairs of other pastors and the churches they represented. It also meant intervening when there was a situation or accusation. I could see in her eyes that this issue was one better done without.

Arriving that night for prayer, the city seemed "closed for busi-ness;" that would prove prophetic. Limited street lights made the place appear extra dark and gloomy. Maybe I would see things in a better light if I had a hamburger, but I digress. One purpose for fasting, according to Jesus, is to be able to expel spirits that could, otherwise, refuse eviction. What we were driving into would demand more than that day's missed meals.

The church porch was dimly lit. I made my way to the restroom to care for our son. I wondered how he'd fair for this evening, but concluded that he had already endured numerous prayer times inside and outside the belly. I entertained the thought of taking him to my sister's house, since she lived a few miles away and is a remarkable mother, but decided not to pull her into the mire.

Exiting the two-stalled toilet, a young lady and I passed each other. She spoke kindly and commented on our baby. Upon inquiry, I related that he was eleven months. He had had his first hair cut that day, and was none too thrilled about the November air hitting his newly exposed scalp. Though no longer outside, it was apparent that the heat was recently turned on, and things would have to warm-up—in more ways than one. We chuckled, and I asked her name. She told me her real name, but revealed that family and friends called her Wa-Wa. *What a nickname!* I thought, continuing down the short hallway that led into the small sanctuary.

Inside were a few members of the fledgling ministry, ushers, and a couple of women perched on pews to the left near the low pulpit. To the right were two pews matching the ones to the left. They faced each other. That room, too, seemed especially lightless, though brass-like chandeliers beamed overhead. Again, maybe it was just me. I couldn't help but notice the royal blue, it was everywhere: pews, windows, carpet. Not that I had an aversion to the color, but as someone who likes interior design, I thought it way too much for the small space. White walls and painted pews were offset by dark wood trim on everything else. There was an old organ to the right. The podium was extra wide and seemed to swallow the room. There I was again, making design judgments. This had nothing to do with me, *right*? So I commanded myself to pay attention.

Our pastor, and their bishop, took one step into the pulpit and opened service. Instructions were brief. We were to integrate and introduce ourselves to each other. In addition, we were to follow along with the prayer leaders already assigned and exchange information later in an effort to continue prayer via telephone. Last, we were to pray fervently and effectually. Pray we did, until lips were chapped and throats were raspy. We prayed for them like they were us, not knowing that they would *become* us.

Service ended. We jotted down each other's contact information, hugged, and wrapped-up to brave the winter's night. I bundled the baby. He had not once cried, blurted, or grown fidgety. He had looked about, played with his fingers, eaten, and fallen asleep. I looked forward to joining him, but knew the long drive home demanded my alertness. Before escaping into the night, our pastor had another request. The Lord had spoken during prayer, so my husband and I were asked if we could return the following Sunday. *What in the world for?* I pondered. As if hearing my head, the answer came: *To minister during morning service.* I had already sensed it during prayer, but promptly dismissed it. We both agreed.

Hours later, it sure felt good to be home. Virginia Beach was no New York, but it suited me well. I liked just about everything about it: the weather, close proximity to other active cities, the plethora of shopping, site seeing, dinner theaters, and dining. Family and friends within ear shot was an extra bonus. Both my spouse and I had matriculated through the local university, so we knew our way about the place.

We were newlyweds, new parents, and new homeowners. In it we installed creamy white carpet with creamy white furniture to match, not anticipating children so soon. But our son was here, and we were all adjusting to an abundantly blessed life. We had made plans, traded dreams, and relayed hopes for our baby boy. He could attend the private Christian school at our church, continue at one of the prestigious universities nearby, and choose any one of the up-and-coming neighboring cities to dwell in—Hampton, Chesapeake, or Norfolk.

"Faith," as we commonly called it, was our church, and it was the place to be. A great deal of our time was spent there. God is the center of our lives, so where we learned about Him and loved-up on Him was vital. Our pastor had sown everything into our ministry, and everyone was reaping the harvest. Thousands passed through the corridors, and innumerable lives were better as a result of it. It was a large church, mega, by most accounts, but if you hung around long enough, faces became familiar, and you'd grow close to like-minded folk.

We were involved in anything that time allowed: Monday Prayer,

Tuesday Bible Class, Thursday rehearsals, Friday "Throw Downs," and Sunday morning (either 8:00 or 11:00) and evening services. In any spare time, we attended meetings, volunteered for the school, and supported our pastor when ministry brought her close to home.

While I was preparing for Sunday's engagement, the telephone rang. On the other end, our pastor had a "last minute entry." Since we were traveling on Saturday to be in close proximity for Sunday, she wanted to know if we would consider attending a private prayer meeting someone at the church had called suddenly. I actually didn't want to be there at all, let alone by ourselves, but we needed to be, so we were.

To say the attendees were shocked to see us is putting it mildly. We rolled our son through the double wood doors and parked his "ride" alongside one of the short blue pews (now twice as bright in the light). The prayer/meeting group, few as they were, was not pleased to see us, and some showed it. I recognized certain faces from two days before, but new people were present to *attack the adversary*. Two or three did acknowledge our arrival with slight head nods, then, refocused.

One woman managed to meander her way to the back where we sat, determined *not* to make matters worse, I guessed. She was cordial and polite, introducing herself as the mother of the young lady who'd admired our baby that previous Thursday. She was Wa-Wa's mom, Towanna. Her genuine greeting put me at ease, making me believe that this might be a good prayer meeting after all.

I'm not sure if anyone thought it was. None of us have ever spoken of that day. Someone opened up with a song. Others joined. I learned right away that Towanna sang. Acoustics in the small space amplified the blended voices, but hers could be heard. Someone else took the prayer lead. By her decisive conduct, I believed that person to be the one who had called the meeting.

During the not-so-sweet hour of prayer, the members were encouraged to walk around while praying and present prophetic messages when they "received" one. They "prayed" loudly and "prophesied" louder. I knew that some of it was to convince us that they were powerful and could make it on their own. I saw the attempt as pitiful, since I had come to know that the power of God cannot be manipulated or manufactured. Two prophecies were of particular interest to me: one came from an older lady who was, obviously, revered by those in attendance, the other by an excited man. I did not recall seeing *either* the night we prayed, so I assumed that they were "back-up."

As service worked its way to a crescendo, the woman sitting in the coveted seats that mirrored each other rose to her feet. The others simmered down, because she was scheduled to talk. I was as focused on hearing what she had interrupted the flow to insert. She rambled on about something that may have been exclusive to them, then insisted, "You will find yourself fighting against God!" *Who,* I thought, *would be crazy enough to do that?* I remembered the famous statement "Your arms are too short to box with God," from the Broadway musical of my childhood. There I was...in New York, again. But this was far from Broadway. This was the narrow road, and there was very little room for anyone not already on it.

The room that day was filled with tension and trepidation. They were trying to pray in spite of us, but invested so much energy into us. The excited man got more excited with the woman's fuel. When she finished, he was ready. His "prophecy" echoed hers. Adding hand gestures, he concluded his with a warning: "Go, go, go!" he said, more times than I wanted to count. He then shifted gears, demanding that someone "Get out! Get out! Get out!" I don't know who or what he was referring to, but I was standing near the back door in the direction he pointed, and I *had* to stay because my pastor asked me to.

I am convinced that some of those present sincerely believed they were ridding themselves of outside influences they perceived had come to harm them. Others, clearly, determined that anyone not *from* them was demonic. Still, there were those who saw themselves as the next spiritual leaders of this scattered flock and wanted no competition.

They had been an entity unto themselves for many years, practicing *their* brand of holiness. Any intrusion was met with suspicion and serious resentment. Many viewed our pastor as an infidel, unsaved and unholy because our church in Virginia "had brought the world in" by praise dancing or allowing women to wear pants.

They were protecting what they had spent a lifetime promoting, and I understood that. I was born-again into that.

Although well meaning, they were misguided. Being one of the "outsiders," I knew what our motives were—we had nothing to gain, nothing to obtain, and nothing to prove. We were not the enemy. Our pastor was commissioned to clean up a mess, so we carried her mops and buckets. No one would escape unsoiled.

Following that sad service, we gathered in the pastor's study for "the meeting." It was to be conducted via telephone because our pastor was unable to get to town before the meeting began. *Oh, no! This was pre-cellular phone, so she had pulled-off on the side of some remote road to place the call from a telephone booth. Since we were already in town for Sunday service and Saturday prayer, we were recruited that day to act in her stead at this pseudo meeting.

"Prayer" had worn me out! Although I had always been aware of the gift I had to discern spirits, the gift was working overtime. Years of quiet on the altar during my youth and the Intensive Intercession during Monday night prayers at Faith Deliverance had sharpened my spiritual skills. I did not see demonic spirits that day, but I did sense their influence and that put me on high alert.

I called my pastor from the study and put her on speaker so that their issues could be addressed. Immediately, things went from bad to worse when my pastor detected a familiar voice. Since I was simply a Sunday morning speaker and spectator, I hadn't been privy to the previous request for this person not to be present because of a clear conflict of interest. It had been decided that the members would speak freely if she was not there to pressure or persuade them. When asked to remove herself from the meeting, she became irritated, initially refusing, then did so reluctantly. She muttered something as she went, and I kept looking toward the phone, as if my pastor could see what I saw.

Acting as mediators, my family sat in the closed, cramped confines of the room with the rest of the congregation, about eight people, as I recall. To remain neutral, we tried not to respond to the stares and sneers of the "saints." What the bishop could not see was their resistance to the plans for moving forward and the rejection. We saw and felt the sting. The final statement could not be made soon enough for me. I said my farewells, shook the few hands that were extended, and almost ran for the door.

There was one notable exception to the severity of that Saturday—the few young people who stood on the porch because the meeting was for adults. Two of them wanted to know, "So, will we still be able to sing?" We weren't sure how to respond, but still laugh about the question. Amid the conundrum of that day's activities, theirs was the comic relief we needed. They didn't know all that transpired, but they knew change was taking place. Unlike the adults, whose primary concern seemed to be their church, the youth just wanted to know if they could keep singing for Jesus? I hoped their pastor would let them. But I had to leave...to pray for real.

CHAPTER 3

I JUST WANTED SUNDAY to come so I could keep my word by rendering the Word; then whist my family back to our comfortable little creamy white world. Sunday did come, but I felt rushed and ill-equipped. I was unsure if there had been ample time to ready myself for what lie ahead. These fine folks did not want us, nor did they feel they needed us. This was the first time I had ever prepared to speak for people who had not invited me. The Lord would have to help me, in more ways than one.

I dressed *less* than modest, like many of the women I'd grown up with. The apostle Paul had taught me to "become all things to all people," and my pastor had advised me "not to take them too fast." I understood the wisdom in both, so lip balm was the substitute for cherry lipstick, a skirt suit for a pant suit, and tiny posts for dangling ear bobs. I felt like a pilgrim, and although there is nothing wrong with pilgrims, I am not one. I had grown up the way I looked that day, but had outgrown what we were taught was unholy about it. Firm in my faith and resting in my relationship with my Father, I knew that looking my best was no sin as long as I consulted Him with my fashion choices.

Months prior to sitting in this pulpit, a ministry engagement had landed me in a church which shared similar beliefs to theirs. As I began to preach, God's anointing enveloped me right away, but I could not put my finger on what was obstructing the overflow. It hadn't occurred to me until I was chided the following week by my pastor for my insensitivity. I wore something red and they found it difficult to see past it. I was so sorry, but had seen something that weekend which was worth my reprimand. The Spirit of God had infiltrated our gathering, tearing down strongholds. People who "sat" on me at first, slowly found themselves caught-up into the glory He initiated; then, they joined me face down on the floor.

After that first night, my husband and I resigned to the hotel room exacerbated. Our plan was to eat, since we hadn't all day, then sleep. What was "on us" entered the room with us, and we neither ate nor slept. We worshipped till the wee hours of the morning, experiencing another realm. It was glorious!

The next morning, though steeped deep in doctrinal issues, no one could deny that God had blessed us despite the *red*. There was so much power pouring into the place that it still remains one of my most unforgettable ministry moments. Miracles, signs, and wonders were prevalent. By the final day, we had become family, maintaining contact even today.

This day, though, I was back in the royal blue sanctuary on Sunday morning. I sat in the too-hard high back chair clutching my Bible and trying to collect myself. People were already there: ushers, the pompous who had claimed the facing pews a few nights earlier, a few men dressed in black, navy blue, or brown, women adorned in their simple Sunday best with matching hats or head covering, and children who stared at me because they had not mastered wearing "masks."

Some light peered through the painted royal blue windows, illuminating faces that furled or mouths that curled. Everyone seemed on their best behavior, as most endeavored to endure this exercise. No music played, since the musician was understandably absent, so clatter, whispers, and salutations abounded. Since there was too much to "hear and see," I took to perusing my notes or playing with the pages of the Word. I could still feel those little eyes, glaring.

A few minutes before the scheduled start of service, the back door opened to reveal quite the sight—the pastor's wife was present and accounted for. Bedecked in "royal attire," bejeweled, beaded and bright, she entered the edifice, escorted. I actually admired what she wore, deeming it more *my* style than the plain apparel I and the other women had on. As she sauntered, my eyes scanned the room, and my mind skipped back to the touchy meeting the day before. This was *not* my call, my care, or my concern, so I stayed myself. I had to preach. Let these good folk and their leaders sort through the spill. I was almost back home.

Following the normal order of service, there was an A and B selection that would be performed by the newly formed youth choir. "The next voice you hear will be that of our guest speaker."

Uninvited guest was more like it, but I appreciated the gesture. The youth group of five stood to the left of the pulpit so I could see them.

Sister Towanna placed them, then took her place before them. A cappella, they followed her fingers then began to croon, "If He has to reach way down, Jesus will pick you up." Indeed He would. There was nothing from that selection to be desired: no pitch, tone, or intonation to speak of, but they had wanted to sing since yesterday. And I admired that. They were not responsible for what happened, and didn't deserve to be pitied or punished, so I applauded. Then, I paused, because I was next.

From the sixteenth chapter of the book of Acts, I took the topic "Midnight Madness" and presented my introduction. The air was thick, tainted, but this was not my first rodeo, so I kept riding. Standing on prayer support from as far back as Virginia, I saw stirring to my right. An usher had come to relay something to the "mother." She rose, gestured to whom I assumed to be her children, and rushed out.

I felt strength and sustenance. Suddenly, things shifted. The struggle was over and something was coming-over me. I didn't rush to finish the message, but I was astonished by its end. When service concluded, my family nodded our good-byes and *stepped-over* people to get out of the room! The Holy Spirit had heard the imperfect praise of the impassioned few and visited our dungeon. Chains were broken, prisoners were loosed, and captives escaped. Moreover, something had been moved and shaken. *Someone* didn't like it.

Now in the van, we praised God for His faithfulness and spoke highly of what He had done. Just a few miles outside the city, my mate and I heard odd gurgling noises. Since there was only one other person present, we turned our heads slightly to check the baby. As soon as we did, he convulsed and regurgitated so violently that it flew passed us, landing on the dashboard and front window. We began to "apply" the blood of Jesus, frantically, while pulling over. As quickly as he had thrown-up, he settled back in his seat as if nothing had happened. One of us cleaned him, the other, the vehicle. We stared at each other in silence, and then returned to the road. Our baby had never thrown-up like that before or since. Strange!

As the road ahead stretched and twisted, we talked. Now, far from the experiences of the past two tumultuous days, we spoke of plans for the week. Never dull, the person driving beside me began to speak less and less. A brief glance caused me to guess that something was amiss. Upon asking, I was merely requested to drive, something he never did. After we exchanged seats, I was only a few feet from merging into traffic when that gurgling sound resurfaced. This time, my husband motioned for me to stop.

The door tore open and the vomit poured out! *What in the world was going on?* I wondered. After a time of cleansing, we resumed the ride, but we would not speak lightly. We had been in enough spiritual warfare zones to know demonic assault when we saw it. This was no virus, bug, or coincidence. We had irritated something, someone. In retaliation, we prayed the remainder of the ride and committed to fast for those "poor people" the ensuing week. We knew this trip had something to do with them, so we set ourselves to fight on *their* behalf.

In Virginia, we reported the specifics to our pastor. We did not include the "road rage" or our decision to fast. We had taken it as a personal assignment and detected that she had heard enough. My family slept that night like we were all babies, secure in the place we called home, under the navy blue Tidewater skies.

Morning came before we were ready, and with it the start of our week of prayer and fasting. The week of activities was nothing out of the ordinary, but that Friday would interrupt the norm. As we sat to break the fast over supper, both of us had the same question, "Has the Lord spoken anything to you?" The "yes" that followed was as long as the word can be stretched. Neither one of us wanted to be the first to reply, so we kept surrendering space to the other.

When we finally compared notes, the answer was apparent. Our agreement to fast for the people in North Carolina was coupled with prayer for God to send them help. At the end of our five days, He was clear, "*You're it!*" From that moment to this, words fail to aid my attempt to express the gravity of what God said. We didn't want to be "it!" And what was "it" anyway? Of that we were unsure, but we were unified in our belief that God wanted *only* our initial response, unveiling the rest as we stepped out with no visible safety net. We agreed to care for the "children" until their parent came.

Our first order of business was relaying the answer to our pastor. When we did, she sat still; then, revealed that the Lord had already informed her. While wrestling with the decision she replied, "Lord, You're going to have to tell them." I understood why she couldn't. It was better that way because when man speaks on God's behalf, it is easier to say "no."

Together, we would strategize over the minutia, as if working from a war room. The overall plan of action consisted of an immediate move to North Carolina, where I would serve as interim minister. Our home would be sold to lift the burden of paying mortgage and rent. Varied skill sets and work experiences should make finding employment quick and painless. The family of Faith was there to support us and our pastor would be available to guide us through any landmines. Plans in heart and hand-in-hand we prayed and prepared for "battle."

Our parents were the next to be told, then our close friends. My mother just wanted to know it was God. She had never known me to move out of turn on such matters, trusting that I'd be sure of the part I heard, first. Her reservations had more to do with her own vision. Once, she had seen the church we were going to filled with blackness, though I never discussed with her the *darkness* that warranted our move. My father just wanted to know if we knew what we were doing, convinced we didn't.

My mother-in-law was more practical, understandably anxious about uprooting our lives and beginning again. We had spent eight unexpected months at her house right after marriage and had only been in our home a short while. During our recent house warming, she complimented us, often, and smiled more than usual. Now, we were speaking of moving. She was concerned, naturally.

My youngest sister was just pleased at the prospect of having me near. We had run-up a considerable tab in telephone calls and longed for what sisterhood would look like up close. Our friends were astonished, taken aback, awe-struck. Despite the sudden obedience and opaque instructions, everyone who mattered was in our corner and would be a few hours away if we ever needed them.

For a time, we traveled back and forth between the two states. Because the King's business demanded haste, we wasted no time praying, packing, and planning. In the process, our pastor was locked-in a battle with the board of bishops who were vacillating between the old and the new. I was determined to stay out of "grown folk's" business, trying only to move at the touch of the One who had tagged me.

> *Ever played tag? After you'd run around, often in circles, trying not to end up in the path of the person chasing you, the touch was always disconcerting. It proved that all of your efforts were useless against someone who knew where you were and saw you running. When they declared "you're it," you knew right away that it seemed easier trying not to get picked than leading. That's why no one ever wanted to be "it."*

CHAPTER 4

Voice of the Fans

HE IS THE *unofficial mascot of many local schools. Showing up for whoever is playing that night; he is familiar to most of us: a die-hard fan with loyalty to the game, only. Tall and stout, he is hard to overlook. Just in case you try, he makes his presence known, often singing as he enters. He waves while searching for a prime spot and speaks to all (even those who don't speak back). This is what floats his boat or tickles his fancy.*

I do not know where he comes from, but he has been here, at least as long as we have, and knows enough about the happenings to work his schedule around all sports' seasons. In addition, he has run for political office various times and been a face in the crowd at many community activities.

I have seen people attempt to ignore him, grow weary of him, and cringe at the thought of him sharing their section. He is different, you see, doing his own thing, making his own rules. Younger fans see him as funny, though he is not trying to be. I suppose that is why he never won an office or is always alone. But tonight, he is surrounded, and like them, he is simply a fan.

One particular night he taught me a valuable lesson:

Seated most of the time, he is not out of order. He leans back in his seat, folding his hands, and then rests them on his belly. He watches keenly. At the appropriate times—time outs, half times, time to rally the crowd for support—he swings into action. Back and forth he paces, urging participation. As a morale booster myself, I appreciate the effort. At the last game of this basketball season, I saw him approaching and readied myself for his antics. He seems to admire our enthusiasm, rarely leaving a game without making contact.

Everyone, at every game, knew he always talked loudly about something. Few cared to know exactly what he said. This night I was bent on finding out, so I leaned-in as he got closer. Finally, I heard what the fan had been resounding for years: "It's a good day to eat at Bojangles!" (a national fast food chain that was not sponsoring the game). I couldn't keep from laughing and the point was well made. As fans go, they can say just about whatever they want...and often do. He is the inspiration for this chapter.

Our pastor put us out there, not alone, but without her. We would have to depend, rely, and learn to trust the One who sent us. She was able and available, but all of her coaching would be done from the sidelines. We were the ones who would have to take to the field or court, putting into practice what she'd taught and running the plays we'd repeated for years.

Her coaching style was similar to the renowned Tom Landry of the Dallas Cowboys or Coach "K" of Duke University. She would be calm and collected until we did something stupid that could cost us the championship. She observed from her place, called us out, gave us signals, and requested necessary time outs. During them, she'd tell us what a good job we were doing, encourage us to keep it up, and demand us to play like a team. At times she'd reprimand us for not using our training, then tell us to get right back out there!

Most players *like* to play; that's why they signed up, showed-up at training camp, and received the bonus portion of their big pay. But this was *not* a game, and I could see no reward worth the work-out. Because my focus was so flawed, I would watch the clock at times I should have been paying attention. Sometimes I ran-out the clock just to get out of the uniform, or robe in my case.

Few people knew how much I wanted to tear-off my jersey, storm-off the field, and talk-back to the crowd, but neither the Owner (God), coach (pastor), or my personal trainer (husband) would accommodate me. They knew that doing so would be considered a forfeit, the enemy declared the victor. So I kept playing, praying someone would put in the second string.

Once, the Owner gave me an illustration for my situation so that I could see things from another vantage point. What I saw helped me then, and now:

I envisioned a football field. The stands were stacked and packed with rowdy fanatics. Both the size of the crowd and charge in the air hinted that this was an important event. The faces on the fans suggested that this might be their Super Bowl instead of the players.

Reporters re-checked their microphones and received last-minute touch-ups while they brushed-up. The players had converged onto the field, working the attendees into a frenzy.

This was what every other game had been about. This was what every win or loss had pointed to. Everything was riding on this event. Money would be messed-over, reputations ruined, and injuries increased if someone didn't bring their "A" game.

Now well underway, the teams were set to run their final play. Exhausted, dirty, and eager, they were one field goal away from victory. Then, from the crowd it came: shouts, insults, profanity, and trash thrown onto the field. It swelled, turning into surround sound, all reminders that the one team was visiting, and the other was home. Music mingled with madness as they pulled out all the stops.

As the visitors, they were calling you names while you tried not to hear them. Stopping to respond would be ridiculous—wasting time, feeding the fury, making you look bad.

They were doing what they came to do: had purchased season seats to do. But you had the ball, and your objective was before you, on the other side of your opponent, the adversary. They were not your enemy. They weren't even on the field, but bystanders. They could not see what you saw, do what you did, or receive what you would. They were the fans, but you had to focus.

With that vision, I caught my second wind and learned to play *my* game.

Because our son was on a little league team and has played a team sport since middle school, we are no strangers to sports fans in the stands. On every sideline it's the same: old mamas and papas who used to play, new moms and dads who think their child *should* be MVP; non-players living vicariously, people who could care less but had nothing better to do, and always, always fanatics who wouldn't run *that* play or take *that* shot. They just wouldn't coach *like that* or play *like that* if they were out there. But they are not! And that's the point.

Fan, I found out, is a derivative of the word fanatic. How true. I've never met a real fan who could not just as easily cross the line to kooky. I am, probably, one of them. We take our son's games seriously, though there is no recognition, reward, fortune, or fame attached to them (right now). A group of us (most, from our church) regularly attend our son's games, usually bringing the color his school has learned to anticipate and maybe even appreciate. No matter, we're fans who dance, sing, chant, sway, nickname the players (White Chocolate, Crispy Crème, Big Ben, Saw, etc.), train the refs, stomp the bleachers, rush the court, wave banners, holler, signify, shake pompoms, correct the coach, and warn *our* players that the opponent "can't dribble with his left, so play to the right!"

Our son's coaches, teachers, teammates, students and a few parents have said that they "love to see us coming." A lot of that is patronage, I'm sure, but most is sincere sentiment. Some parents have, jokingly, offered to reward us for bringing the fun or becoming the fan-base for their shy kid.

Sports fans are a blabbering bunch, but the fact remains—after the many noises and voices, the best players are the ones who pay very little attention to either. They are able to distinguish the voices of *their* coach and *their* team. Those are the only voices that should determine their choices. Between the pep band, painted students, pacing mascot, shakin' cheerleaders, screaming babies, bells and whistles, megaphones, and clamor from the kooky crowd; that must be the *real* challenge. The ones who *master the mania* might just win.

The people I was sent to assist were not my fans, but the Owner had traded me to their team, and we would have to learn to work together before we could win...and walk away with the prize.

CHAPTER 5

Characters Welcome

EVER SEEN THE popular television show "Honey Boo Boo?" I
hadn't, but a friend introduced me to the idea and urged me
to watch. When I did, I was intrigued right away. An apparent
spin-off from the programs that followed the lives of tiny pageant
princesses and their overzealous parents, this show is set in some
southern town and features the real life goings-on of Honey, and
her hysterical household.

"They just plain folks:" farting just for fun, sleeping with the pet
pig, smelling each other's breath to pass the time, scratching where it
itches, dumpster diving to shop for goods, and doing serious damage
to the English language. Their cozy country dwelling may not be fit
for HGTV, but they tend to have a better time being around each
other than *any* of "the housewives."

I liked them right away, sitting through more than one episode
during their "Boo-a-thon." On this night, a hungry Honey asked
her mom to prepare her favorite meal. To the request, "Mama" rose
from her soiled seat, passing stock piles of can goods and household items. Clicking and clanking, she found the needed pot and all
her essential ingredients. They consisted of: angel hair pasta, tons
of butter (you can use margarine), and as many squirts of ketchup
as the microwave bowl could hold. With licked lips and tomato
stained hands, Honey Boo Boo was pleased with the cuisine. I was
"rolling," and guilty of spending too much on my spaghetti.

I especially liked the main character because she is just that...a
character. She is honest and hilarious, rounded and rambunctious.
She speaks her mind, even when her words aren't perfect. She snaps
her fingers and rolls her neck. She plays to the camera, but is not pretending. She isn't mean, but mouthy, the kind of kid I enjoy in my
company when I've been given parental permission to "help them."

Honey Boo Boo is a hit, and I can see why. Most people aren't
this raw or real. They have practiced pretense so long that the curtains never close, the credits never roll. They are performers and

puppets, placed somewhere and made to move when cued. Boo Boo's people are just *being*. Their real life characters are enough to keep people coming back.

Early ministry paraded a cast of characters before me: the mentally challenged guy who tried to steal a kiss when I went to shake his hand, the brother who rented out our car as part of a drug deal, the woman we found praying in the literal closet of our church, the quiet man who faked fainting to disrupt service, the student who was late for Bible Study because he had just hit a bear, the person who fell asleep standing in the prayer line, the acting soldier who whipped our Jesus for real, and the young man whose rap included enough expletives to shame his mama.

Speaking of cussing, for my birthday one year, my husband and his committee planned *quite* the surprise. On that Sunday, it was announced that a special guest was coming forth to bring the morning message. I was pleasantly surprised to see someone rise from the back row, where she had been hiding behind everyone else. Dr. Lonise Bias is the mother of the legendary Lynn Bias, who was drafted to play in the NBA and decided to celebrate his contractual agreement. His life would, tragically, end that night as a result of a drug overdose.

Before the conclusion of his overcrowded public funeral, this grief-stricken mother was requested to give some final remarks. Since the Eulogy had already gone forth, mama Lonise turned her attention to the thousands of youth, professional athletes, coaches, and owners who were not promised tomorrow. Within minutes of taking the microphone, there was not a dry eye in the building, or heart that had escaped her piercing reminder that death is not biased, but that the Giver of life was granting eternity to all who received Him. Those words launched Dr. Bias into the national spotlight and powered her personal mission to save young people, one life at a time.

She and I had met years prior to me becoming a minister. She made an instant imprint. Her height, upright stride, stern countenance, and stage presents were palpable. But the words she worked into parable and parody were without warning. God had graced her with a knack to draw an audience in and take them wherever she needed them to be. I invited her to share in more settings, including on the state and national levels with the organization I grew-up

in. At the conclusion of one event, she turned to me and set forth
a preposterous rhetorical question before exiting, "And you: when
are you going to stop playing and preach for real?" I pondered her
question for the rest of that meeting, then released it as heretical.
Where I was from, woman shouldn't entertain such notions.

Now, standing before our small congregation, I considered how prophetic her words were. A gifted orator, she began to walk us through
this *special* tribute. I sat in the beloved side pews to her left, resting
my leg beside the man who worked hard to bring this birthday delight
to fruition. Before closing, and with little warning, Dr. Bias took note
of the number of youth present for this occasion. The observation
caused her to do something so unconventional, it crossed all lines of
protocol and proper etiquette. *None* of us were braced.

Stressing the need for youth to distance themselves from the wiles
of the enemy and filth of the flesh, she let a cuss word or two slip, or
so I presumed. After she strongly opposed the damaging lyrics in
songs that our youth knew all too well, she commenced to dispel-
ling the belief that they were innocent and nonthreatening. To prove
her point and convince the stunned parents, she borrowed a few for
effect. Then, more! And, more! One *blank-a-de-blank* after the other
passed her sacred lips! With each, I squinted, adults shook their
heads, and my husband sunk in despair. Was this birthday going to
"hell in a hand basket?" I'm sorry, was that cussing?

New to ministry, I sat trying to figure out, *fast*, what would be the
most tactful way to handle the situation. Then it dawned on me, this
was my *husband's invitee*, so let the program coordinator handle it!
Later, my husband shared how shocked he was, initially, then humiliated, then disturbed. He said he couldn't resign how so much preceding prayer was ending in a pathetic presentation. Finally, she rested
her case. But before taking the seat we *wanted* her to find, she dared
to follow the "street performance" with the good of the Gospel and an
altar call. I was even more astonished, but this was a day for surprises.

I prayed under my breath, not wanting her to be left standing at
the altar. I prayed for myself, since she had mentioned turning the
service over to the birthday girl for final remarks. I prayed for our
church, that something salvageable was probable. Then, to my utter
amazement, one young person after the other made their way down

the aisles! *What!? Were they in the same service? Had they heard something I didn't, or not hear something I did?* All of my training and theology were being twisted. All logic was thrown out the blue tinted windows. Dr. Bias prayed for each of them, taking her time, hearing their hearts. *They* had heard *hers* and were *not* offended.

My remarks were ever so brief. "Had I known that all I had to do...to get you close to the cross...was cuss ya'll out, I would have done so a long time ago!" We all laughed. Now, I have never used profanity, but that experience taught me a profound lesson: *the Gospel,* not a person, is still *the power* of God unto salvation. This was so far from the norm, but the Gospel had neutralized service and saved the day!

That "who would have thunk it day" was not the last or the most memorable of my early ministry experiences. All of my pastor friends seemed to deal with more *usual* issues, but we had enough drama to take our show on the road. At times, one would have thought the circus was in town because so many acts centered around church folk. Another such situation unfolded across the street from where I sat and would demand that *I* play a role.

I was working in the fellowship hall of our church because the claustrophobic study had no windows. Doing my normal ministry things, I prayed at the altar, studied the Word, returned calls, set meetings, and checked the lists of things still left to do before our first church drama. A series of knocks from the side door broke my concentration. On the other side stood an out-of-breath young lady from our ministry. She had run across the road to get my help. As I was briefed, we galloped towards their house.

Inside the foyer was her sister, standing before a closed door. After they conveyed the particulars, I shouted to the occupant on the opposite side of the solid structure. "Hey! This is Elder Wellington. How are you doing in there?" I began.

"Not too good!" the voice came back, shaking and stuttering.

"It's okay," I assured. "I'm gonna get you out!" *One way or the other* I thought.

The old lady who owned the house and insisted she remain when the new family moved in was no stranger to anyone in town. She had been a permanent fixture: fancy, forked-tongue, and, reportedly, financially well-off. Today, private and sometimes paranoid, she had locked herself in her room and could not find the key to get out. She was frightened, to say the least.

The other residents had tried to pick the lock and even spoke of breaking the door, but, were discouraged by the trapped old home-owner. She was adamant about not wanting to ruin *her* house. I presumed she wouldn't take too kindly to the idea of busting through the roof, like the friends in the Bible. So I scratched that thought. I chose to do what any other respectable reverend would...*climb through her window*!

A man named Jack Miller was my usual volunteer look-out, who often kept vigil from his front yard between sips of *spirits*. I wondered what he and his tipsy friends thought of my visit to the "shut-in" this day. Since I knew how panicked the lady of the house was, I told her the plan in advance and asked her to look for me. Now well up in age, some people thought she showed signs of dementia, so I restated who I was and what I intended to do. It's good I did.

We ran around the side window near her bedroom. I stepped over debris and other items she refused to discard. I climbed onto something that led to something else. Now close, I tapped the window, which startled her. From without, I reminded her who I was and asked her to come to the window. She starred at me too long, and then wheeled herself over to where I was. "It's me, Elder Wellington," I stated again. She pulled herself up, and then worked to unlock the old windows which were painted shut. I just stood there, talking her through, reassuring her that "every thang is gonna be alright." I sure hoped it was.

Tapping and rattling the window loose, I raised it high and wiggled my way through. *Wish I had on pants right now.* Of course I considered what this might look like to passersby, but a minister had to do what a minister had to do. I worked my way into the room, falling onto her too soft bed. After a brief roll, and continued communication with her, my eyes landed on the object directly beside me. It was a *hand gun*! This didn't feel good. Was she contemplating the unthinkable, preparing to harm herself or someone else? Caught between a rock and a hard place, I hugged the old lady tightly, putting space between me and her piece. When I asked about it, she simply said that she "never planned to use it, but always carried it wherever she went…just in case." She was in our sanctuary the previous Sunday. Her piece didn't give me peace, but I let her out, anyway.

No one would know if they met Honey Boo Boo on the street that she was a pageant contestant who had more than enough trophies, crowns, and prizes to her credit. Years of grooming, training, and practice had prepared her to participate. Character prepared her to win. She knew exactly when to "bring it" and when to take the make-up off.

Honey Boo Boo was at our church this past Sunday, *so to speak*. While meeting in a local hotel upstairs, downstairs was one of those little miss pageants. The girls of our ministry could hardly wait for us to get out of a meeting to inform me. "Hey, guess who was here?" they teased, out of breath.

I'm game, so I countered, "Who, little boo boo's (a common term of endearment within the African-American exchange)?"

"Honey, Boo Boo!" they exclaimed.

I became more excited than they were. "No! When? Where?" I said while picking up my pace to find her.

"She was in a pageant in the room downstairs."

"Well, is she still there?" I replied, still moving.

"We'll check." They went in the direction of the elevator. While they ran ahead, I tickled myself. What must I look like—a full-grown former campus queen going to see Honey Boo Boo?

I slowed my roll, remembering how unimpressed I usually am with celebrities. But that's the thing. I know quite a few celebs—important people, famous folks. That's not what drew me to this irregular crowned princess; it was her character, not the one she *plays*, the one she *is*. The people I was sent to help were sort of like that, characters in their own right. What they were not was pretentious; they were simple, home-grown, down-to-earth, modest, and committed…all characters I welcome.

Driving away from the hotel after my Honey Boo Boo hunt, I smirked. *I might want to be like her when I grow up*, I thought, *knowing when and how to "bring it," but having the best time just being myself.* Character is the combination of qualities which make us unique. I prayed our ministry would find its distinctiveness and not ever be ashamed to flaunt it. You're welcome!

CHAPTER 6

It's Official

I HAD SURVIVED THE first year! As was the agreement, I awaited word from "higher-up" concerning their decision. It came via telephone and was not what I expected or was prepared to hear. The board had concluded that the old pastor should not return, but could begin again somewhere else. "Excuse me?" I exclaimed. "But what would happen to the group I had *temporarily* shepherded until their pastor came?" It was strongly suggested that I continue feeding the flock since there were signs of growth and development. I was shocked and shaken, needing time alone.

I made some of this needed time, taking my grievances, disagreements, questions and concerns to my daddy, God. "Crawling up in His lap, looking up in His face," I sat quiet. I did not want to do this anymore, and only He knew how much I meant it. I wanted out, felt burned-out. That season had been sufficient. We had been to "hell and back." I believed I had *earned* the right to exit stage right, or left, it didn't matter to me.

The church *still* had a new mortgage. The home we left *still* had a new mortgage. We were broke, with no money in a church account to receive a salary, stipend, or love gift. Most members were underemployed or unemployed, so I was "paid" with produce or, on special occasions, chicken sandwiches. My husband, who had never been unemployed until then, had numerous temporary jobs. On one, he simply showed up at the designated spot to see if he would be one of the manual laborers hired for that day *only*. Many more positions were applied for, with little to no activity. The ones that did respond spoke of over-qualification, always adding how sorry they were. But sorry didn't pay bills, give groceries, fill the tank, or purchase Pampers. When I could no longer shop at the area Wal-Mart, I looked for shoes and clothes at the Good Will. I was resourceful, but I felt sorry for us.

For the first time, though not the final time, we knew what it was to have things "turned off." We were stretched and stressed.

My husband, the lighthearted, was not acting like himself; he was moody, seldom sharing, bothered. Though I had grown up poor, he had grown up lacking little. Out of those two camps came our various responses. Waking up to puddles of water on our bedroom floor or swarms of termites in our kitchen stunned me, but didn't sidetrack me. My husband, on the other hand, seemed distant, dismayed, and disappointed that he was unable to handle his business.

I never blamed him, choosing to call myself the culprit for getting us stuck out here. He refused to play the blame game, reminding himself and me that *we* had sought and received affirmation *before* this move. We had a promise attached to our obedience, so provision must be forthcoming. We hankered down, in hope, because we were in this for the long haul, as one.

During those times, God allowed just enough support to supplement our short-comings. The first happened while preparing to travel for a ministry engagement. Towanna asked if we had a minute to meet her at the church. She knew our schedule, assuring us that it would only "take a minute"—a statement that has become her mantra. When we arrived, with absolutely no money and little gas in the tank, she was not there, but a white envelope was.

My husband retrieved it, stuck inside the doors. By the look on his face, I knew it was good news. She had given us our first love offering. It was thirty dollars, an amount that seems exorbitant, considering how indigent she was. We drove away, thankful. My heart was enlarged by her gift, too, because the act demonstrated that we were beginning to love one another. I was no longer the person pushing her way in.

That small token of appreciation would go far: with it, we were able to eat snacks from home and pump enough gas to get us all the way to where we were going. The conference blessed us, and my mother's cooking filled us. And neither giver was privy to our predicament. There was nothing lacking, nothing missing.

Speaking of an envelope, there was the time we were asked to meet with the Sr. Lewises. The brevity of the meeting was obvious to all parties involved, since it was scheduled to take place immediately following service. Most people knew of our need to drive to the neighboring city, unwind, then return. At their home, we were offered drinks and asked to make ourselves comfortable. On the sofa, we sat across from the husband and his wife. They had both been present during that whirlwind of a weekend when we first arrived.

As the wife began speaking, I couldn't help but remember how angry and opposed her husband was to my appointment as interim minister, refusing to come back to church and keeping his son home with him. Since that time, he had humbly begged my forgiveness and wanted a fresh start. This day, he sat a few feet away with something on his mind. He yielded the floor to his wife first. I'm not exactly sure if she got it all out, because the phrase I heard had something to do with the Lord telling them to empty their bank account. I listened more carefully, not having a clue where this was going.

They had received foreclosure papers and were preparing for the worst. While praying, they believed God had laid-out their financial strategy. "Empty your account and give the money to the new minister."

Pardon me? Now, of course I knew the story of the Biblical "bake-me-a-cake-first" woman, but this was going too far, as far as I was concerned. "If you want to save your house," I reasoned, "take the money from your account to your mortgage company and work out a deal!" I refused to be a part of a family being evicted. I knew what that was like, *personally*.

Shaking my head, while they tried to push an envelope our direction, my husband spoke-up. "Thank you. God bless you." With those words, we prayed and rose to leave. The three of them hugged and grinned—as if striking-up some sort of successful agreement. I wanted to agree with them, but I was worried for them, and us, for taking the two hundred and forty dollars. They must have heard from Him because a miraculous chain of events would allow them to stay in their home and pay less than before. In addition, their money would be restored. They are still in the same house these fourteen years later.

Then there was the "bag lady," not because she was homeless, but because she brought a bag to church one Bible Study night. After class, I decided not to collect an offering. At that time I was so sensitive to the struggles we all were enduring that I thought it would help to forego giving. I knew what the Scriptures said about God honoring sacrifice. I just assumed that this turnip had no more blood to give. I was not only wrong, but disobedient. I had sided with the world's theory of keeping the little you have until you get more, instead of giving so it can be given back.

I wasn't the only disobedient one that night, but I started the ball rolling. Days later, Sister "bag lady" Annie asked if she could have a moment of our time. I postured myself for the possibility that she might be the next to exit, since the situation that brought us to town had caused similar casualties. Then too, she was not one for meeting if there was no real reason. My husband and I met with her, giving her space to speak.

She was a curious type, not easily understood. She was shy reserved, conservative. But *anything* she did from the pulpit transformed her into another person. Wholly committed to God, she lived by the Book, and stood for little foolishness. She seldom gathered in clusters and didn't have many friends, but had been loyal to the ones she had for years. She was soft-spoken and direct. New people weren't sure how to approach her, but if they dared, they would find kindness without measure.

I wasn't sure what she thought of me because we were different in almost every way. I had noticed her smile *once*, as we prepared to leave for Conference. Everyone was waiting in front of the church as I emerged from the building. They were all astonished. I had survived my year of head coverings, chapped lips, and more-than-modest apparel. That day, I was free to be *me*: multi-colored silk top, fuchsia lip gloss, and curly, spiked hair. Sister Annie could not maintain her normal stoic composure. I had made her smile, though shaking her head, and I considered that making progress.

The day we met, she got right to it. We were to receive something she believed the Lord wanted her to give that previous Bible Study. She planned to include it in the offering, but *I* had selected not to take one, so *she* chose to keep it. She said she was scolded for her disobedience, probably the same time I was for mine. Now back to set the record straight, Sister Annie took-out a Glad bag full of bills and handed it to us. We stared at it. I remembered the Lewises, so

I tried not to mishandle the moment. Not one for hugs and kisses, she said, "Okay, I've done what He said," and left. I didn't know everything about her, but I was positive that if God had "use" of her eighty dollars in a bag, she was glad to give it. I had to trust that it was, indeed, "better to give" because I was overwhelmed to receive...especially from the lady with the bag.

Towanna, the Lewises, and Annie were "winks" from God that we were going to be all right...*all of us.* I was careful not to try to gather sympathizers, so no one knew how little we lived off. *No one!* Since the saints didn't know of our struggle for simply sustenance, they had to be susceptible to the Spirit and willing to stretch what little they had when *He* directed. We were all strained to sustain basic needs. But there is something about struggle that either binds you together or tears you asunder. He was binding us. We were helping each other within, and receiving help from without.

It was one of those days when there was more month than money. The church had little, and we had less. We had exhausted all savings, investments, and reserves. Our systems of support failed. In the mail that day was a substantial check from Dr. Tessie Jones, a co-laborer and friend of our pastor. In her prayer time, she had "seen" our faces and could not shake them. Thank God! We were astonished and amazed that God could put us on someone's heart and refuse to erase what was there until they acknowledged and obeyed.

Also, there was the time we walked into our apartment and were stunned by the telephone ringing. Of course, they are made to ring, but we had not paid the bill and ours was disconnected. My extended family had paid for us because they loved us too much not to be able to reach out and touch us.

That experience reminds me of another. Before we answered the call to ministry, we returned to our Virginia Beach home to find the light switch not working. We stepped in further and tried another, and another. Nothing! My husband continued to "click," as if the first few didn't take. I removed my purse and moved towards the kitchen. Seeking my secret stash, I took out cleaning supplies, then spotted what I needed. There, tucked away *for such a time as this* were my trusted kerosene lamps with fresh wicks. Behind them were candles and a small box of matches. As I worked to prepare them, I could hear my husband still searching for the answer and saying something under his breath. I think he made a call to the power company, but I was busy empowering us to have light later. "Okay!" I heard him heartedly proclaim.

There had been a power outage in our area, and the lights would be back on shortly. "I knew there was something wrong!" he said victoriously. "I pay my bills!" In fact, he did—on time, orderly, obviously. His credit was impeccable, squeaky clean. People wanted *him* as their co-signer, though he knew better. Companies wanted his business. His integrity had afforded him privilege. His conduct commanded honor, even from the much older men at the multi-million dollar facility he ran for the federal government.

But this is not the government: this is the ground floor of ministry, ground zero. There are no designer offices, paid vacations, spit-shined shoes, time off, or housing allowances. There *is* sweat, nights without sleep, and silent shrills. Some advice goes unheeded, some messages fall on deaf ears. No one knows your name, and few care. Anything that goes wrong is your fault; anything that goes right is short-lived. But there was reward coming, Jesus reminded, "in this life" that would outlast a lifetime.

Although we had grown up differently, my man and I would have to meet in the middle, sharing similar stories. I now believe this was one of the primary purposes for our pathetic start. My husband knew what having was like and could only sympathize with the have-nots. He would be compassionate and caring, but only because he was already that. What personal suffering provided was empathy, the ability to identify with other's situation because *you* had lived it. I do not believe God *made* us impecunious or penniless. Most things were bad before we arrived, we made our own mistakes, and things could have been done more efficiently. But we would minister from another angle, guided by greater grace and much mercy after we lived through our own lack.

It's amazing what a simple "yes" can do. After fussing and fighting, wrestling and worrying, tossing and turning, a single "Yes, Lord, I will," made the struggle subside. He had been calling, but kept getting my voice mail telling Him to leave me a message. At times, I did "pick-up," but just listened. Now, I answered "yes" before He would ask again. Already licensed and ordained before coming to North Carolina, I was officially installed as the new pastor in February of 1998. I wore copper-colored pumps to that auspicious occasion. Not yet silver or gold, but I had been tried in the fire and began to turn into something of greater value.

Family, friends, and faith filled the crowded blue church to turn this big page with me and my family. They bore gifts, brought greetings, extended blessings, and dined sufficiently. Then, as with all such gatherings, they packed their vehicles and left us standing on the porch. We were now legitimate, but alone.

Mothers feel the same about their child's first day of school.

He storms the steps, skipping a few. He is dressed so cute: teeth brushed, hair combed, laces tied. He is in high gear—running, jumping, spinning. Breakfast is not the most important thing this day, school is. He has waited for this his "whole life", and you are the only thing thwarting his progress. Still nit-picking, you look him over again, making sure he hadn't missed a spot. He is antsy, so "Just forget it, Mom!" On the drive to school, you can't help notice his shaking foot and tapping hand. He stares out the window and wants little discussion. The car is not moving fast enough for him.

In front of the school, you go to let him out, but he is a big boy now, so he beats you to it. With a miniature book bag and Batman lunch box, he runs in the direction of the building. You catch up, insisting on walking him in. The woman with the eyeglasses, who you met two nights ago, greets him with open arms. With that "All right, you've been here long enough" look, you retreat. In the van, you sit for a moment, then look back before pulling off. On the long five-minute drive back home you wonder: "Should I return to eat lunch with him? Is he going to be all right? Have I forgotten something? Will he know what to do if I have? Will he meet friends? Is he ready?"

Our son survived his first day of school and is now a high school honors student. In the days between that day and this, he has forgotten his lunch, done projects at the last minute, and come home with scars. He must have been ready.

None of us knew if we were, but class after class, lesson after lesson would prove it. Sometimes we'd attend, other times we'd be absent. Sometimes we'd do our homework, other times we'd forget. Sometimes we'd follow the book, other times we'd improvise.

CHAPTER 7

By The Book

IMPROVISATION WAS SOMETHING we found we were good at. We had gone so long without so many ministry tools—like money—that we could work with almost anything. We learned that we were imaginative, innovative, and industrious without really trying. Even now, we are considered to be "that creative church." Creativity was really the byproduct of nothingness, much like the Creator stepping onto the edge of the abyss and announcing "Let there be." Calling those things that were not, as though they already existed (Romans 4:17) became our standard operating procedure.

Our first venture was a drama written by my mother, which we hoped to perform beyond the walls of worship. Thinking outside the blue box, we held auditions, selected actors, distributed lines, and began rehearsals. You would have thought some Hollywood producer was in town by the high activity surrounding the event. *Everyone* in the ministry had a part to play. Almost all of us were actors in it. Those who weren't sewed, made props, painted, or babysat.

After a few promising practices, we had the audacity to ask for use of the local high school and embark on an advertising campaign. Now that the cat was out the bag, it took little time informing us that we were wasting ours. With no precedent, area residents told us not to expect much, because "people around here don't attend things like that." But attend they did, young and old alike, to applaud our effort and approve our anointing. They would support whatever dramatic presentation we performed from then on, packing the place and looking forward to the next one.

Drama played a primary role in most of what we did back then. My husband would re-enter the church as a Roman Guard after interrupting his own class to welcome our "special guest." He would return in his previous regular clothes, and people would still be looking to see where the other guy went. So funny!

One visiting dramatic group would ask how high our ceilings

were before they could commit. Their ministry didn't include just singing, but acrobatics up and down our tiny middle aisle! You can't make this stuff up! Our adult Sunday school teacher would dress-up in costumes related to the subject. We had a passion for the dramatic and discovered that we were gifted to transform almost any program from plain and boring to fantastic. All would be done in unconventional, unlikely ways.

The Praise Project was introduced to us by a group doing a university study on diet and nutrition. Unveiling their vision to provide fresh produce and healthy meals, we jumped at the chance. A free well-balanced meal went a long way during those days. In addition, we decided to augment their version with one of our own. We followed their procedures, provided their data, then took the opportunity to give their idea a "kick." We had an International Food Festival, presenting servers from other countries with their complimentary cuisines. My husband was Frenchy, the Parisian chef. We decorated the tiny fellowship hall with foreign flare and tasted foods from other countries and cultures. It was fun, fun, fun!

There was Bus Stop Breakfast, which fed local children while they waited to catch their buses; Sidewalk Service, when we turned the church inside out (having service on the front lawn); and "Happy Being Me," an all day grooming, hygiene, personal care seminar. We were finding our niche, our "thing." At the time, I didn't realize what a blessing we'd been given until I'd go to other functions and imagine what the program would be like with a little intervention. I always wanted to interject what I thought might enhance the ordinary. Event planning came natural to me, providing a break from some mundane ministry matters.

Having traveled to our parent church on numerous occasions, our young people liked what they saw and wanted to emulate. I introduced praise dance first. Mime, step, and rap followed. They enjoyed it so much, rehearsing anytime, anywhere. I attended *every* practice, determined that if we were going to do it, we would honor God and do so with the excellence He deserved. The all-day, late-night repetition was sealing our bond, as well as sharpening our skills. We still share something special. Rehearsal, for them, meant polishing their praise.

This proved to be their way of loving God, giving back what He'd given as an offering. I taught them that, drilled it into them, because I never wanted them to see what they did as performance, but worship for an audience of One. At that time, no church in the surrounding area was providing a forum for their youth to do the same. Most are now. Many asked our assistance in getting started or staying on task.

As much as we were finding our footing, there were those waiting in the shadows to trip us. Some insisted that I opened the door, allowing the world's ways to walk their halls of law and order. Our ladies encountered "sanctified spies" who would say that dance was from the devil, and I was doing his bidding. And if dance didn't destroy us, denim pants would. But, I kept right on because I had been cleared for take-off by the Pilot I was committed to please. Everyone with me was bound for another place. Dance and denim would be allowed *there*.

Something had been nagging me, the proverbial knot in my stomach. I had attempted to rid myself of it, but it would only lessen, then return. Each time I went to read or study the Word, the same scripture showed up—not suddenly appearing, but rather my eyes falling on the same verse in different books. Even references about totally unrelated topics would lead me to the same verse or verses right above or below it. Then things got more perplexing. I would hear it in sermons, on the radio, in other reference material. When I mentioned it to my husband, he stunned me by stating that he meant to tell me something similar. He was having interesting encounters with the same verse:

> "And if anyone will not welcome you or refuses to listen to your words, shake the dust off your feet."
> —MATTHEW 10:14

I wasn't sure what it meant as far as I was concerned, or what I was supposed to do with it, but I could not shake it. When my eyes fell on the same verse one day, questions ensued. "Was this about me? Did this have something to do with *our* ministry?" But we had come so far, survived so much, and my soul was *finally* "settling." That may have been the issue. I was smug in a situation that was supposed to be temporal. I prayed for revelation and any information that could determine a proper course of action. The answer came in a most unlikely way.

One Sunday we had visitors, as usual. But there was something curious about this group. I thought I recognized one, but didn't have time to contemplate. Something about them reminded me of the strangers we had last week. We would learn later that they were working in concert, in cahoots (sort of like those spying out the land). They said nothing, just sat and played along until the power of the Highest overshadowed us and hovered over our service. To that, they stood, clapped, nodded, and responded to *the truth*. Play time was over. They had apparently been blessed.

Immediately following service, they introduced themselves as representatives "from the top." One was an attorney and wanted to speak privately. We took our time sending the saints away and met alone. While engaged in small talk, my husband repeated where she, the attorney, stated she was from and shared that his grandparents lived in the same city. For some unknown reason, he also added their names. She visibly responded.

Astonished by the names, she informed us that my husband's grandparents were clients of hers and had been so for years. With that, she lightened up and calmed down. By the look of the load she bore, a long meeting was planned, but she forewent the formalities. Succinctly, she wanted to question our style of service, suggesting that it may not be *in line* with the doctrine, or dogma of the denomination. I asked "What part, in particular?" For that answer, she wanted me to refer to the handbook which, it seemed, took issue with just about *everything* we were doing. When I asked, "What handbook?" she saw her way clear. "They didn't give you a handbook?" she retorted. At my "No, ma'am," she gathered her items and concluded our meeting. She included that she would relay her findings and suggested I request a handbook. Translation: You can't break a rule that *only* exists in a handbook you were never given.

Now it all made sense, the two secret guests from the week before *had* been sent to spy out the land (though no Joshua or Caleb). They must have taken back an evil report and gotten the crowd all worked-up. A second reconnaissance team would have served us notice, but the book got in the way. It always does.

CHAPTER 8

Dusty Feet

T HAT'S WHAT THE Bible calls them—dusty feet. They got that way carrying the good news on dirty roads while exposed. In travel, followers of Christ sometimes came upon someone who would rather not hear the Gospel or entered the home of someone who didn't want what they had. They would be misunderstood and mistreated. Jesus forewarned His disciples of such situations, and then instructed them not to make a scene, cast dispersions, or throw stones when it happened, but to simply shake the dirt from their feet and keep it moving.

Jewish scholars of that day knew exactly what Jesus meant because it was a common practice and jargon. When guests entered the home, the host was obliged to offer water for washing the feet that sandals hadn't protected. That fact explains the famous washing of Christ's feet by the long-haired worshipper with her costly ointment, and the foot washing service following His last supper.

Though for different reasons, it is customary today to offer your guest, at least, a glass of water. Since Jews believed that you picked-up something from everywhere you went, they didn't want any contamination from a place or the people there to attach to them. Shaking the dust was a prophetic gesture signifying separation. In addition, anyone treating company so poorly that they denied them water would be ill-treated themselves. Not bestowing hospitality upon a guest was worthy of a curse, or, at the very least, cause parting of ways.

It became abundantly clear to me that we had worn out our welcome. We were working too hard to get most in the area to accept our version of church. At that time, there were those who didn't even want a national food chain because it might make them too big and too busy. Where was I? For the most part, people were never rude to us. They just kept their arms folded. They were good ole folks who liked our dramas, but didn't want our ways. Also, what they didn't know was how much I was holding back in an effort not to rock the already shaky boat.

As far as the organization, we were trying too hard to get them to like us. They knew we were not like them. Many were decent, docile sisters and brothers who meant "heaven every step of the way." Most were not cruel or calculating, but they were calcified, set in a certain mold. We did not fit, no matter how much I tried to "beat" our puzzle piece into place. I refused to call names, point fingers or tell them a piece of my mind, though they made what was on theirs quite clear.

They were doing what they believed was right, and I was going too far in the opposite direction of their position. What we did and who we were becoming was not in the infamous handbook. I could not keep pretending, perpetrating a fraud. I could not keep breaking *their law*. I liked the colors God made, even on my lips, and I liked pants made for me. We liked dancing before the Lord, and we liked stepping to offer our praise. Together, we liked illustrated messages and out of the box occasions. Staying and fighting would have cost all of us far more than it was worth. That was the source of my nagging sensation, and I was the physician who had to heal herself.

"When you don't know what to do: do what you know" has always been my philosophy. I knew I should fast and pray, so I did. I still wasn't clear, but the same impression intensified, "Shake!" Seeking relief, I spoke with my pastor. She knew right away that God was calling us away. The dam broke! I began to cry because she confirmed what I had carried, what I had covered. I thought I was off, had missed the mark, was "in the flesh." *Was all of this in vain?* was one haunting question. The other, *what would the people do, now that they had come so far?* I didn't know, but *I* had to go! The God who brought them where they were would never leave them. The God who brought me there would never let me remain.

My pastor blessed me and my family, praying that God would continue to order each step. She released us, praising our good fight of faith. She walked me through *how to leave*, trusting that the news would not destroy their faith or love for God. She would handle the issue of transitioning them...again.

I hung the telephone up and experienced immediate consolation. My husband *already* knew what our pastor relayed, had sensed

it and said it. But her corroboration meant moving on into the
unknown. Move! Neither one of us wanted to hear that *four letter
word*. I didn't know how my mate could be so calm and not see this
as some cruel joke. He had given-up the most, in my opinion, but
continued to obey. He is my hero!

We had endured that test and been blessed. But the reality of
breaking the news to the remnant was daunting. I did not know
what would happen to me or them. I only had the first step.
Someone described faith as standing on the edge of everything you
know, then taking one more step. One foot was set in what I knew—
the other in the air. I was braced to cross that line of uncertainty.

That Sunday's service was like none other! We had worshipped
and waited until there was no more room in the habitation we
built for Him. The Lord was in His holy temple, filling it. The
atmosphere was sweet, soothing. Simply glorious! Only now am I
recalling that it was reminiscent of that sermon-less Sunday when
we were "called" into the office at the church in Norfolk.

In the Spirit of the house, I could not minister the message I'd
prepared. It would be an unnecessary interruption to try and take
us where we already were. I closed my Bible, folded my notes, and
sat in His presence. When He was done, we planned to dismiss.
Before releasing the assembly I asked to meet with members, only,
directly following service. The anointing in the atmosphere had
emboldened me to address the apparent.

I spoke slowly and methodically. I began with my love and like
for them. Next, I summarized our journey and celebrated our suc-
cesses. Feeling like our Lord must have in his final hours—trying
to get it all in—I reiterated what I wanted them to remember most.
I challenged them to Love God with all their might, never passively,
ever passionately. Then, I forced the words out, "Today is my last
day here."

The fallen countenances were worse than I'd thought they would
be! I could not speak. The room remained still and deathly silent,
as if someone had turned off the volume. Sobs broke the barrier,
sighs followed. Then, a hand rose from the back. I just nodded
permission to speak, because words escaped me. The young lady
stood to project. Her small, broken voice asked one question, "I

just want to know where you going, 'cause I'm going wit' you!" I started shaking my head, but it was too late. Someone else stood near her, saying, "Me, too." Others chimed in until everyone in the room was standing, on one accord. I was flabbergasted! This was not what I anticipated, not the plan. Or was it? Proverbs 19:21 states: "Many are the plans in a person's heart, but it is the Lord's purpose that will prevail."

Those present pledged their unity and proposed a temporary plan. My husband and I would secure a meeting space and call everyone with the particulars. Driving the destitute back road home that afternoon, we just stared, occasionally repeating the same, "What in the world?" I wasn't sure of *what* just happened, but it didn't seem to involve returning to Virginia Beach. I supposed we were staying...though I didn't know where or why.

We cleaned and shined that little blue edifice like we would have wanted it to look for our coming. I notified the proper authorities and locked the double doors for the last time. I never looked back, not even physically. I've always been anointed to be done when I'm done. The prized key was mailed.

Our Egypt was in the rearview mirror, but "pharaoh" wasn't finished calling, stopping by, making accusations, or presenting propositions. We were done, but he, she, or it was not. "Yul Brynner" would play the part until well after the fact! The Bible relates that pharaoh had a change of heart, after coaxing, and assembled his army to take back what, or who, he presumed belonged to him:

> While cozy, encamped by the Red Sea, the sudden sound of hoofs could be heard in the distance. They were terrified and paralyzed. Weren't they told to go? Wasn't there an agreement? Hadn't all parties involved suffered enough? Didn't they do things by the book? As bad as things appeared in the rear, this final showdown might prove to be the most important.
>
> Cloud coverage, courtesy of God, had been providing protection from the elements by day and served as their night light. Now, in broad day light (because He wants your enemies to see what He can do), it would move from over them to behind them, preventing pharaoh from just rolling up on them. Still too

close to slavery not to be scared, the children huddled together and looked to their leader for guidance. Apprehensive, Moses didn't have any answers himself, but knew who did. A brief discussion with the "I Am" revealed that the prince of Egypt was equipped with everything he needed to take them the rest of the way. The cloud would hold enemies at bay, but Moses would have to learn to use what was in his own hand. The Lord would talk him through how.

Steadying the rod stretched over the Red Sea, Moses must have been shaken and unsure, himself. All miracles he had seen God perform involved contests between the gods of Egypt and the Almighty. This incident could end in mass murder. But he steadied his hand and held the staff until something happened.

With nowhere to go but straight ahead, the sea surrendered her strength, splitting wide open! I'm sure Moses wanted to pause a moment to take in what had just happened, but there was no time. The clanking of weapons and clamor of frightened followers joined with wind and waves. No commands of what to do were needed: the way was obvious, so they stepped in.

What they stepped on was another matter. This wasn't messy mud, slippery slopes, or patches of puddles. Under them was dry! They wouldn't even get their feet wet. As amazing as what they were walking on was what they were walking into. There were no wet walls according to the Biblical account: water was solidified, congealed. Israel could not fail, so they had to ignore the wall, look straight ahead, and keep walking forward. Forward was imperative because any one could just as easily walk back, turning themselves over to the pursuer, giving up.

I and those following me could have given up too, but going back was no option. As with Israel, God waited for the last one of us to reach shore, and then closed the sea behind us. Not only were enemies drowned, but there was no possible way back, even if we backslid. I often wondered what those who murmured in the wilderness intended to do if Moses had granted them leave. What was the plan when they got to the Red Sea? And did they think pharaoh would be glad to see them? Surely God closed the back door for a reason.

We were sort of baptized in our last sea, something drowned with each step. Our feet hadn't gotten wet, either, but some debris from the sod we trod could still be on us. We would have to shake it off on the other side to be sure.

The Lord, according to Scripture, took the children the long way around because they couldn't fight. Not that they had never been in a fight, but the struggles of slavery had left them whipped. Just imagine, not one of them had successfully attempted an escape or coup? As slaves, they had never learned to fight, and that training would be necessary every leg of their journey. They would have to fight to stay together, fight the temptation to look back, fight to move ahead, fight to get so close and not be anxious about what they could see before them.

She was running late for dinner. Pulling into the parking space, she lowered her mirror to refresh lipstick and fork through her hair with her fingers. Inside the restaurant, she scanned the room, then proceeded to follow the greeter to the man standing, looking her way. He'd remain that way until their gentle kiss and warm embrace. Motioning her to be seated first, he listened to her carry on about the unexpected which caused her delay. He forgave her before she even said anything because he knew her and loved her anyway.

Their daze was disrupted by the waiter, who had already met him. In his hand was a strawberry virgin daiquiri, whipped cream atop, with a side of pineapple and kiwi. She knew it was hers and thanked her date. The waiter set the tall glass down and placed the napkin in her lap. His only question: "May I get you anything else, this evening?" The man across from her spoke up before she could, "We're good. Thank you."

She did not question, override, or grow confused by his reply. She knew him. They had shared innumerable meals, and she knew his ways. So she excused herself to practice personal hygiene, and then returned to pick-up where they left off. Servers suddenly showed-up bearing two plates. The wife smiled, her husband winked.

He had ordered for her.

Taking the liberty, he had commissioned her favorites. She could trust what he ordered, because he was well acquainted with her likes, tastes, allergies, and aversions. They were in covenant, sharing everything. So, not only was she pleased he had ordered...she was allayed. He could go ahead of her and order for her anytime. If left up to her, she might still be trying to decide.

Descending Dove Christian Center would begin walking, but every step would have to be ordered. We could trust His unfailing love and His attention to detail that would determine what came with each "meal." God pays for everything He orders!

CHAPTER 9

Numbers

O N JANUARY 18, 2013 I read this scripture as part of my personal devotions: "And the children of Israel set forward, and pitched in the plains of Moab on this side Jordan by Jericho" (Num. 22:1).

With the words of that one verse, I ended my reading, taking up mechanical pencil and notepad. I felt compelled to write because *their* words seemed to provide summary of *our* journey. I had not wished to write before: perhaps it was too painful, the idea too immense, or I thought too much of what people might say. But I have outlived my concerns and know enough about seasons to seize this one.

The words *set forward*, *pitched*, and *on this side* proved poignant. They explained, in essence, both where we *had been* and where we *were*. By *we*, I mean me, my family, and the ministry of Descending Dove Christian Center, the name we became.

We were a small band of men, women, and children who traveled from a place called Mount Sinai (in every Biblical sense) in search of the place God promised. Because of the parallels, I have often compared our journey with that of Israel's. We had endured religious task-maskers and bondages. Suffice it to say, we were elated to be free, but could not have envisioned the cost of that liberty or length of our wilderness. We set forward. And we were out there waiting on God to do something, at times *anything*, to prove He was still with us, and we were still with Him. Chains had fallen off me, too. But with the new freedom came the new reality that I was, somehow, responsible for finding us shelter and safety. We had shaken the dust from our feet and set forward, but backwards was, at least, familiar and stable.

Our first stop outside pharaoh's city limits was a local hotel. We set-up the speakers, chairs, podium, and microphone; then we prayed that the glory we were used to experiencing would fill the room. Desperate for Him, He came, and we left full. I remember a message I ministered in those days, "I've Traded in My Raven for a Dove," because it spoke of our recent name change (Matt. 3:16). Again and again, we set up, He showed up, and the room filled up. Obviously, our volume went-up and the hotel quietly asked us to leave because guests were complaining.

At first, I was hurt and anxious: hurt, because we were not so much as given a warning; anxious, because we would have to begin…again, again. The people of our ministry had helped to build the new little church we left. They had scraped and strained for years to raise funds for their edifice, and now they were "homeless." In addition, I felt shame and humiliation, believing I had let them down for not providing pasture, and let God down for presenting a poor witness to the people at the hotel. What I could not have known then was that we had set-up shop and tried to act normal. And we, DDCC, were called to be far from that.

There would be a number of stops, slight turns, and slow paces as we went: hotels, schools, conference rooms, lecture halls, hallways, science labs, restaurants, lobbies, clubhouses, parking lots, vehicles, parks, backyards, homeless shelters, nursing homes, gyms, libraries, dance studios, game rooms, choir rooms, board rooms, events centers, business centers, a recreation center, a lodge, a golf course, a movie theater, a housing project, the city council chamber, the hospital chapel, other churches, each others' homes, via conference calls and computer monitors. Yes, we have met, worshipped, rehearsed, gathered, prayed, or celebrated in all the above.

I'm sure I left out something, but our longest stay was on a university campus. What started out as a two week stint became our tent of meeting. There was excitement in the air upon our first visit. It was Bible Study, and I was teaching from the Acts of the Apostles. With the new study materials, overhead projector (tee-hee), and our classroom alongside other evening classes came the news that an NBA team was there practicing and training. We felt special, somehow, included among the academic, athletic sort. Perhaps we were glad not to be hidden in the woods or held-up within the walls of a church structure. We were still in the wilderness, but it had light, and we were it. We so wanted to make an impact, or at least an indent.

As we set forward, there was no real way of looking forward. We could not know, discern, or imagine that our stay on campus would not yield the dividends we'd hoped. The numbers didn't add up; no influx of people, no impressive offerings, fund-raisers, or gifts. Oh, sure, we had enough visitors to make a church, but they came and went and, more often than not, the ones that stayed had so many needs themselves that we were ever-giving.

Once this very prominent looking fellow stopped by and still speaks highly of us to anyone who will listen. He was so moved by what the Lord was doing in our midst that he vowed to send us an offering upon his return home. We received it, all twenty-five dollars worth. Joining him were other pastors, bishops, rabbis, activists, artists, politicians, producers, promoters, professors, physicians, school administrators, teachers, coaches, and entrepreneurs. One millionaire commented that, in his opinion, we were "the best kept secret in town." Perhaps he wanted us to remain that way.

Remain that way we did. But I wanted results—lines out the door, offerings that exceeded every expectation, ministry that could be measured. I desired tangible, visible, undeniable proof that God had, in fact, called and sent us so that any critic, skeptic, or cynic would be silenced. My hushed yearning revealed an ego screaming for acceptance from people who may never approve and peers who may never affirm.

Though unspoken, the seed of pride had surfaced, and I knew it was merely a matter of time before Holy Spirit would dig deep and uproot it. Getting to the root of anything is never easy or pretty. What was planted is disturbed, things that were hidden are exposed, pests scurry in the light, and often you hit something else that was buried for years. And since the process is seldom done in one day, the destruction is laid before passersby to see the unfinished project. Such was the soil of my soul. I would experience many seasons on this journey, and with each came the need to be hoed, plowed, sowed into, and gathered. God, the Giver of seed-time and harvest, knew how to grow us. He seemed to care a great deal about what we were *inside*, not just our size.

I recently heard a prudent teacher (my husband) convey that contests to grow the biggest fruit or vegetable have less to do with substance than size. He explained that the emphasis is how big, not how good. By comparison, he suggested, "our churches are in competition to get bigger, but what's inside is often not edible." The numbers on the scale may be impressive, but no one is better as a result of it. The farmer poses for the photo then loads the monstrosity on the back of his pick-up, adorned with its new ribbon. Back at the farm, he feeds it to hogs!

Let's be clear, we are great proponents of extending and expanding the kingdom of our God. We delight in children being added to His family and are fully committed midwives. We, too, are certain that any living thing should grow. What we reject is the focus on bigness *above* discipleship. We want to be growing "in Him" as our numbers do.

People, even shy people, like going where there are a lot of other people. It is the reason we say things like "Everyone's going to be there." Although virtually impossible, it sounds appealing. Who wants to be the only one left out? If there, I can meet someone special, find a friend, show my new clothes, see what others are wearing, network, and not spend Friday night alone. Moreover, I'll be able to report that *I was there*, in the likely event that anyone asked. Church can be the social spot these days. I'm not so sure that's wrong, in and of itself. It stands to reason that the people we gravitate to the most share our values. But that shouldn't be our *only* reason, or *primary* reason, for attending a church.

I can also understand the desire to blend into the background of bigger ministries. In the church we came out of, mixing in with the multitudes was a comfortable position for me. Being called to the forefront meant having to work, sacrifice, and be inconvenienced. At Descending Dove there was no place to run, no one to hide behind. All hands were needed on deck. Everyone's skill was required. Membership meant you had to multitask.

Our group had no outward growth to speak of, at that time. But if cracked open, members would show growth and development off the scale. We are not yet thoroughly "cooked," but are clearly being transformed. The way we took was helping to change us from the inside out. We were not the same people who left the plains of Sinai. With each baby step, we were becoming His children…like the *children* of Israel!

The book of Numbers is a curious bit of writ. I used to wonder why God included it in the Bible and agreed to the name. Upon further investigation, the thirty-six chapters render much more than their name infers. The census, or counting, of Israel takes a backseat to the main point: that being, the final leg of their journey before entering the promised possession and receiving the promised inheritance. The last verse restates their position before pressing in: "...unto the children of Israel *in the plains* of Moab *by* Jordan *near* Jericho" (Num. 36:13).

The point is well made. Though they are poised to possess, are on the mark, and set to go forward, they are still *pitched* in the plains, *sitting* beside Jordan, *facing* Jericho. Everything God said they could have is just a river and a rampart away.

CHAPTER 10
Campus Life

THE BOOK OF Numbers relays a familiar story concerning the spies sent to search the promise land, their reports, and the fall-out that follows. It is the proverbial straw that breaks the camel's back and the place of no return. God's patience has been tried, His goodness taken for granted, and His plans rejected. As a result of their constant complaints, He has made a decision...to proceed *without them*, allowing Joshua and Caleb to usher a new generation to their new home.

From that biblical account, I have been so careful not to complain, with my mouth or *my heart*. Though He has taken us the long way around, I am clear that it was for *our* good and *His* glory. Our longest time pitched on a university campus provided the greatest opportunities for growth. Though not ideal, our time there was inspired.

Sometimes the rooms were too hot or too cold. Sometimes someone forgot to schedule us, so we sat outside, waiting. Sometimes we got too comfortable, then had to relocate for the holidays. Once we arrived on campus to an empty room because they were renovating and someone failed to inform us. On that day, we were rerouted to a meeting place across campus and had to redirect all members and visitors as they came.

When we finally got started, we realized that the room was where we began years earlier. It was now painted all black (floor, walls, ceilings). Though dark, dismal, and dank, *God* made it holy ground. We thought the name of the place, King Hall, was a sign, since we were always seeking a navigation system.

That day was memorable for me for another reason. Our family moved into a new home the day before. After moving and renting and moving and renting for years, we were given the keys to our *own* place. My husband had worked long days and, sometimes, laborious jobs to surprise me with this creature comfort. I was so grateful, to the point of being giddy.

The circle seemed almost complete, but I had a difficult time resigning how *we* could have a house and God's people still be pitched in a tent. Though we had given up our first home to accept the assignment to ministry, I could not discount the thought that members had, too, given up *their* place. Thankfully, that is *not* how they viewed it; they genuinely rejoiced with us about our home, as if it were theirs. After church, members commented that they perceived the news of our move as opening doors of ownership for their future homes (few of whom were homeowners at the time), as well as being part of the restoration for things we had sacrificed to stay in the Carolinas. That reminds me of something.

Years ago we rallied the members of our ministry to assist a single mom in moving into and renovating a home she had been given. Now the fact that it was a *gift* should have alerted us to its condition, but nothing could have prepared me for the degree of work necessitated. My husband and I decided to stop by a day ahead of schedule to devise a plan. From the outside, there were immediate concerns for the decorator in me. But the pastor pushed passed it. Inside, the situation called for more attention than our unprofessional cleaning crew could bestow. We agreed to return the next day, regardless.

Early that morning, we prayed, then set-out to flip the house! It was not easily turned over. With bandanas, plastic gloves, and bedraggled clothes, we set ourselves to make the place livable. It was old and dilapidated, but the trailer the family moved from was overdue for demolition. We *had* to make it work.

Everything required scraping, scouring, soaking, or sanding. Linoleum needed to be pulled and replaced. Appliances were covered in soot, badly stained. You could see through gaping holes under the floor and in the ceiling. I had to close off one room because wasps had made themselves at home. My husband used the paint machine we rented to spray the entire interior a neutral shade. As a design team, we wiped down, washed, polished, primed, and worked to exhaustion. People had donated time, items, and attention to help make this house a home. That was far from our last housing project. Over the years, my family would pack, move, paint, and decorate for other members because that's what families do.

I am so blessed by that reality, but rest came one day while reading the account of King Solomon's building project. When God allowed me to see how He favored the king having the house he desired *and* approved his temple building plans; I realized that God, the Builder, was still on site, and we were still on schedule. No one else could have shared that with me and settled me. I began to decorate.

While I decorated, the university planned to renovate and wanted us to relocate. This time—*indefinitely*. Like the new pharaoh who didn't know Joseph, a new administrator was not fond of the idea of our utilizing their facility for worship. He issued a moratorium, informing us that "the university was shutting down to all outside organizations until further notice." We received the news prior to leaving for our annual fellowship conference in South Carolina.

Arriving in Beaufort, I struggled to switch into "church mode" since I didn't know where we would meet the day after conference ended. Surviving similar situations, I found my praise place and prayed for another miracle. Before the night service concluded, my mind had made its way to where we were, and all was well. *But the night was young!*

After service, we found old friends, hob-knobbed, chatted, and chewed. We then boarded the bus and looked forward to well deserved sleep following a very long day. Fortunately, directions suggested the hotel was close. Unfortunately, it was not what the hotel had promoted. Against the advertisement, it was a motel: deceptive and decrepit, with soiled bedspreads, blood stains on sheets, rat traps in plain sight, visible bed bugs, water bugs, broken air units in July, and bath tubs that hadn't been cleaned.

As if that were not enough, the one recalcitrant desk clerk took hours to process check in, and after multiple calls about additional room issues, refused to let us check-out with our refund. Our bishop arrived with the local pastors in tow. They had come to assist but by that time, everyone was returning to the bus, determined not to stay at "motel hell." Since the title *pastor* should never be confused with passive, suffice it to say, we left—with *all* our money.

Faith Deliverance Christian Fellowship Conference proceeded with glory and power. The hosts were gracious, the bishop was profound, and the saints were blessed beyond measure. The conclusion of the conference was so stirred by the Holy Spirit that chairs had to be moved to accommodate the resident anointing. One young man traveling with us was saved, healed, and filled that night. He had former gang ties. One of the women in our group was so transformed by the word and demonstration of power that she returned home to inform clients and distributors that she was out of business. She was a former drug user and dealer.

The Lord had done such magnificent things for us that I almost forgot it was Saturday, and we didn't have a place to meet the next day. Not many people knew that, so the bus swelled with laughter, stories, music, and memories of faith and fellowship. In the front, I sat praying and peering out the window, pondering what to say, and when. Then, a message was sent to me from the back, "One of the places we contacted called back and we could use it tomorrow!" *Thank You, Lord*!

Our church that Sunday was The Executive Center. Sounds special, huh? I suppose it was, located on the upscale end of town near shopping, dining, a golf course, and gated community. It was also attached to the area library, so any noise had to be kept to a minimum and was carefully monitored. One thing I have looked forward to for years is the freedom to *shout* unto God with the voice of triumphant!

After months, the moratorium was lifted; an "insider" informed us of this, not the university. We were allowed to return, but not before meeting with a board of administrators. They were a serious sect, set-on separating the church and state. Within minutes of opening the meeting, the combative atmosphere shifted in *our* favor. Whatever was planned was thwarted as we spoke. Miraculously, without enacting their new policy, the decision was made to grant us the honor of returning and resuming, and to allow us to begin paying from that point on. Initially, it was suggested that we pay for years of prior use, *or else*. Favor is better than finances, and we had much more of the former. Hallelujah! Later, we learned that the obstinate "pharaoh" of our previous moratorium wouldn't be returning. We remained.

Riding away from the meeting, I replayed the board's resolution to charge non-profits based on the wear and tear of their facility.

I chuckled at the thought of how difficult to impossible that must have been to calculate. Deciding how much of that wear and tear was inflicted by students and how much by outsiders must have been arduous. When we first used the auditorium we normally met in, it was nothing to be desired for looks and little for function. It was dated, seats were broken or missing, cushions were badly stained, and desks were riddled with graffiti or profanity (our son learned his first cuss word from the seat in front of him during church).

The carpet was filthy, the walls needed painting, and there was always trash left over from whatever happened before Sundays. Some of that, allegedly, included a white supremacist group meeting in the same place we did. So in addition to having prayer an hour before service to clear out anything unlike God, we were mindful to use a cleaning committee before service and when we concluded. Taking the advice of our mothers, we always left the place like we would want to come back to it.

With the moratorium now a meeting away, we returned to campus. The absence had made us grateful to be anywhere, but keenly aware that this was not our home. We were sojourners. Setting feet inside the newly adorned Morton Hall, Bryan Auditorium felt so out of the ordinary. By most observers this was an average renovation, but it seemed extravagant by comparison. There was new carpet, new seats, new equipment, new paint, a new smell and no trash for us to discard. I saw it as cute (and now, expensive), but nothing to get comfortable with. That had already been done, and then the "cloud moved."

With the newness of the place, we started new things. Word Works was a talk show style service where we interviewed guests or introduced the Word in dramatic form. We made good use of the new lobby furniture, too, working it into a set design and producing special graphics for the three new screens. Honors Days were included, inviting community honorees for us to make-over. The Dove endeavored to do everything with style and dignity. Birthdays that year were extraordinary; in a state-of-the-art theater, we walked down memory lane, turning various other rooms into life scenes. Everyone returned the following week to solve the mystery of our dinner theater.

Christmas seemed to come too early that year (2011). As the

students were busy about, taking final exams and loading up parents' hand-me-down cars for the holiday, our surroundings became still and somewhat somber. I knew we would soon have to leave, as they closed campus for the holidays. We had rehearsed this ritual many times, but something seemed strange. I didn't think we would return to this place again. I'm not sure I wanted to. But not returning would mean one of two things: someone else's place or another pit stop. Neither "Potiphar's house" nor "the jail" seemed like viable options to me. Campus was no longer a prospect either.

One day after we "graduated" from the university, someone asked the question we had grown to despise, though it was seldom asked maliciously: "So, where are ya'll, *now*?". The reaction to the news that we were no longer on campus elicited unexplained excitement. Had we missed something? What they shared was that certain people would never feel comfortable joining us for worship because they viewed the campus as "too white" and uninviting. The fact that we had been there may be signs of change, but the people born and reared in the area didn't want to deal with *that* devil. Even if misinformed, we now knew why it was *so hard* to get them to cross what they deemed the invisible color line.

Children's Church

THE CHILDREN OF Descending Dove Christian Center are the true Joshua-Caleb generation. I have heard many youth groups compared to the Old Testament duo, but only theoretically. Baby Doves, King's Kids, and G-Clique have personified the names and earned the title. They are not perfect, by any stretch of anyone's imagination. But they are youth who have spent most of their childhood in a wilderness, of sorts, and have not complained.

They have prayed as hard for a new church as any adult. Our own son has thanked God every day and night as a toddler, tween, and teenager. Most children of our ministry have not regularly attended a church because they were born after we left the only one we had together. Birthed outside of "Egypt," they have trekked this road alongside us. The babies who were "passed-out" on pews when we started with sunrise prayer are now preparing for college.

Since they are not bound to any particular place, they never think inside the box and function as a church without walls. For them, it is not a slogan, but real life. Because they have grown-up between where we've been and where we're going, they are not haughty, snobbish, or proud. The good of not being birthed before the "wilderness" is that they are not children of law or bondage; they are grace babies and free! Thank God!

Freedom is God's idea, and children exemplify that without trying. After most services, meetings, or rehearsals, they were forced to remain until their parents were done. For fun, they would entertain themselves by running around, making-up silly games, throwing anything that resembled a ball, and dancing. They liked to dance, *and could.* We had taught each of them that God granted the gift of dance and wanted them to enjoy it, *with Him.* We explained that it was never to be vulgar, inviting, or glorify self.

On more than a few occasions, the parents would emerge from meetings to find them all over the place, laughing, on the loose, and loud. Little of what they did was wrong. They were simply being young and free. But no where we were was home. Besides what it might look like to the casual on-looker, I had to remind them, constantly, to keep it down. I was hypersensitive, almost paranoid, about *how* we could be perceived. We didn't need another eviction.

Once, one of our little children managed to pull the fire alarm to "find out what it was." As we walked to our vehicles following Bible Study, sirens, emergency vehicles, a fire engine, and campus police made their way to where we were standing. How embarrassing! Our children pointed to the culprit and laughed all the way home.

Also, when we became hopeful about the use of a new facility, one of our children decided to "count the knobs on the office doors" when one opened. Within was a woman whose decision to work during her weekend off worked against us. She was livid, to say the least, and probably shocked to see someone fall into her office. Though we had agreed to pay up front, her report caused the events center to cancel any additional use. That child was scolded, sorry, and scared, but the matter had been decided. Neither the manager (who had acted as if we were the best thing since white bread) nor the owner ever returned a call, accepted an apology, or responded to further request... to this day. Some things are too obvious to utter.

What I will say is that at the time the building was secured for use, the owner was out of town. He had never seen or spoken to us. Our administration dealt directly with the manager. The place was so new that few people knew it existed, so our using it was welcomed. The manager did mention, before we exited, that the owner viewed tapes upon his return, and although he had no other complaints, we were cast out. I wondered what else he "saw?" What he must have seen was more than a twisted knob. *He saw us.* We were hurt, but "the cloud" still hovered overhead, so we stayed under it.

If our church children ever felt denied or deprived, they never said. The parents: not so much. Some parents visited our ministry once or twice, but concluded that there was not a lot for children to do. Others never bothered since we informed them, before hand, that there was no Children's Church, play land, toy chest, game room, mocha café, computer lab, day care, after school, or Vacation Bible School. These were amenities that neither time in someone else's space or resources would allow. We always informed parents that their children would learn to love God, talk to Him, and live for Him.

As a parent, I understand the desire to draw our children to God by any means at our disposal. We just didn't have that luxury. Ours was an anointing to be innovative, inventive, and imaginative. I longed for the time when our children could enjoy the goods that children of other ministries have become bored with. More importantly, I never want them to forget Who matters, most.

I love children! All shapes and sizes, colors and creeds, personalities and perspectives. They are the spice that makes life palatable. I especially love The Dove children. Each of them is gifted, sharp, and loaded with possibility. Many make me laugh and melt my heart. Some make me want to see *their* children. Others make me believe that they will take what they've been given to better the world. They were taught that none of them has a little, insignificant Jesus while adults have a greater brand. They were trained to lay hands on the sick, tell someone God loves them, pray about anything, and thank The Giver for everything. They were trusted to be Children's Church, not just go to one.

CHAPTER 12

Guess Who's Coming to Dinner?

BIBLE STUDY WAS about to begin, so my pace across the asphalt was swift and steady. The lot filled fast on week nights as students vied for premium parking space. Since everyone was bobbing and weaving, I didn't pay much attention to the Caucasian clan closing in on me. They passed, entering the same building. Now walking and waving, I entered the auditorium through the door that gave me access to the front.

When inside, I acknowledged those present, then adjusted my podium. Suddenly, it struck me! The same white people who passed me in the parking lot were sitting in our seats. Perhaps they had the wrong room. Perhaps they had the wrong night. Perhaps someone should tell them. As I looked for a courier, clarity was provided. This was not a single group, but various believers who had, unwittingly, decided to visit on the *same* night. People from our ministry who sat near them extended greetings, a fact we would later be told made quite the first impression. One gentleman, confidentially, conveyed that no one at his own church had ever welcomed him. What a sad indictment.

I commenced with the welcome, invoked God's presence, and began the new series on "God, the Holy Spirit." What none of us predicted that night was that they'd be back the next week and many weeks to come. That is far from the best part. They would bring their family, friends, and pastor. Yes, their pastor! And he would bring his family. He received our hospitality, ate at our table, and encouraged his members to continue the meal. I have never seen or experienced any example of authentic servant-leadership like his. In one act of loving-kindness he added to my life in ways heaven will have to repay.

There are people who come to your table by invitation or incident. You have scrupulously cleaned, shopped for specialty items you think they'd like, labored in an overheated kitchen, and decked

65

the table using your best ware. You are sweaty and somewhat
stressed, but determined to make sure they have dined sufficiently.
Moreover, you want them to leave having felt right at home.

Some guests picked through the food laid before them, but
ate only polite portions while others ate everything, as if heeding
their grandma's command to clean the plate. The latter was
always to satisfy grandma, not oneself. But there are those who
come, sit, want all they see, eat all they get, and go back for
seconds.

Such were the guests who came to dine with us. They were greedy,
wanting anything and everything Jehovah-Jireh provided. I felt
obliged to continue serving the best I could prepare and He always
blessed the meal. On the menu, at that time, was the biblical account
of the early church being baptized in the Holy Spirit. Because He was
part of the main entrée, He was always worth waiting for, present
each time we gathered, satisfying us time and time again.

One night at the end of eating meat, I was led by the Spirit to invite
anyone wanting more to drink. They did. And what happened next
can only be credited to what was *in* the meat and drink, not the server.
The Holy Spirit descended like a dove, lightened upon us, and filled
us gently, sweetly. There were no chairs or tables overturned, no fits or
raging, no foaming at the mouth, and no screaming or screeching—
just a precious, undeniable, unforgettable presence. It was marvelous!
We left in quiet, though some of us wanted designated drivers. Still
lofty, it should have been illegal to drive in that state.

What began as a Bible Study ended as a study in how the body of
Christ *should* operate. One year after they came to visit, our guests
had spent each season with us. Now it was time for them to "go into
all the world," giving what they had received and serving what had
satisfied their longings. Just days ago, someone informed me that one
of the teenagers from that time is on his way to the mission field. Now
Spirit-filled, he has more to share than a meal from the states, he has
the Drink. Many others would follow them, coming to Descending
Dove in search of something from God, then returning to their
churches, communities, and diverse corners of the globe.

They came for the experience that cannot be refuted, replaced, or remanded. They left us with hope, hearts that were opened, and healing for wounds we never knew cut so deep. We all became fellow laborers, prayer partners, and even friends. We would learn from and lean on each other, laugh and labor, cry and celebrate, worship and wait. We would eat many dinners together, both spiritually and naturally. They would come to know us, and we them, simply because we sat down at the table to eat.

It would be awhile before I came to know the series of events that led our guests to the table. I had been asked to speak at a Women's Retreat and invited the women of our ministry to come along. They were always supportive, but this time I wanted them to be exposed as well. The retreat, you see, was sponsored by a church which had a Caucasian congregation. I knew our women would have no apprehensions about fellowshipping, but I felt the new experience might prove beneficial for both entities. I spoke on two days. Because someone was blessed by what was shared the first night, they asked some of their men to invade our gender-specific gathering the following morning.

Among those in attendance were two people who played such essential roles in blessing us that we are still the recipients of their favor. One was an older man who interrupted the end of my sharing to say something. Not knowing if he was crazy or criminal, wanted to debate or disrupt, I still agreed to allow him words. *What was I thinking?* I reasoned, after it was too late. What he wanted to do was apologize to me and the women with me.

He began to cry while explaining that he came, reluctantly, to see for himself what all the fuss was about. He pre-judged me, the message, and my motives. He had thought and practiced racial intolerance, not often showing the love of Jesus. But God's Spirit had arrested him, and he needed to beg *our* pardon. After requesting forgiveness, he extended an invitation for other people who believed like him to do the same. He had an additional request. He wanted permission to shake my hand.

I granted it, but hesitated. He came forward, with an outstretched hand. We shook; then, he opened his arms as if he wanted an embrace. I grimaced. Years of divide and distrust swept over me. Things I'd suppressed surfaced. Things I'd buried revived.

All movement in the room stopped. Faces were dripping with tears. Even I found it hard to see through the well in my eyes, or speak. So I just obeyed the still, small voice that doesn't need repeating. *I hugged him back*! I never recalled being that close to *any* white man, especially not one who just articulated his recent angst about me. Then, I felt it; the unexplainable release of tears, torment, and trepidation. I did not hate him, I didn't even know him.

I would see him again, though, in that Bible Study—the one where black folk and white folk ate at the same table. He and others from the Women's Retreat followed the aroma of something good being cooked, so they showed up for dinner. It was good to see him again. Glory to God!

Then there was the unnamed woman. She, too, was present at the retreat. That night, I introduced a young lady from our ministry as my daughter whom I had asked to learn praise dance when I first became a pastor. She learned, thrived, and was as committed to that call as I was to mine. She was appointed as head of our dance ministries and is now the owner of her own dance company.

That night, though, she was just the little lady with a big gift and a small issue: small because it *could* be resolved, but big because it was costly to do so. At the time, we didn't know how much. The issue was her teeth. This beautiful, gifted, sincere, vessel of honor danced with all her might, but often with her mouth closed.

At some point during her presentation, someone saw what was inside and no longer wanted her to hide. Within days of the retreat, a woman I wasn't familiar with contacted me to ask permission to "bless our child." I promptly explained that my reference had a spiritual connotation, not natural (though any parent would be pleased to claim her). The young dancer was not my real daughter, and her own mother loves her deeply.

Now clear, she commented that the offer would still stand, since I thought enough of the praise dancer to honor her in that way. The proposition was short and astonishing: "The Lord spoke to me, and I have enlisted the assistance of a few friends. Together, we agreed to fund all the work necessary to create her smile and are committed for as long as it takes!"

"What?" I said out loud, then repeated it a few more times to confirm. "Are you sure?" I resounded, because I refused to have her elated, then deflated. "Can I tell her?"

Her reply, "Yes we are very sure, and yes you can tell her, but we *never* want her to know who did it. God will know."

He knew how much our family had desired to do the same for years. This would not just be the desire of her heart, but ours. The unidentified woman and her secret sisters remain that way until this day. I pray that the Giver of every good and perfect gift has granted those individuals willing people who care for each of their children as graciously as they cared for "mine!"

They kept their vow to God, and our "daughter's" $40, 000 smile can be seen from across a crowded room. The work took many years, countless medical visits, endless braces, and multiple oral surgeries. This past Christmas found her at our table, and I couldn't help but smile at the great gift smiling back at me. We are all so grateful, and she is now a gorgeous young lady…who smiles while dancing.

A few words at an intimate retreat produced restoration, renewal, refreshing, and reconciliation. We were their guests then, and many of them would be our guests forever. The breaking of bread together is nothing trivial. It is so imperative that Jesus would make a big deal about sharing a lad's lunch on the lawn, looking forward to the last supper, and a fish fry after His return from the dead. One of the first things He wants us to expect when we see Him is the Marriage Supper being held in His honor.

There is something God is "getting at" when He calls us to dine. It is far more than sitting in close proximity, passing the plate, and minding our manners. It is fulfilling the joy of the Invitee, Who wanted each person present to partake of what He paid and planned to give. He is delighted more in feeding than we are in eating. And every child around His pot is receiving what is good to and for them. We could eat in our rooms, alone. But He makes more for the multitude than individuals. Like a good parent, it fulfills His joy to see all of us sitting around the Master's table.

CHAPTER 13

The Colored Vote

CAUCASIANS, AFRICAN-AMERICANS, ASIANS and Latinos sitting together must look more like Heaven than today's church. Descending Dove was once included in that celestial number. About the time we were ending our "gray" (not just black and white) Bible Study, we were invited by a local pastor to join his church in a multi-cultural, multi-denominational, multi-gender call to prayer. On the heels of a hopeful exchange, we relished the idea. We, too, had practiced a life of prayer and looked forward to how God would honor our oneness.

We gathered monthly for all night prayer and were "up" for it. Long before we did anything else, our church prayed. We prayed before the sun came up, conducted noon day prayer, and even had some midnight intercession. Our earliest prayer services consisted of us dragging in before six, sometimes with scarves, slippers, and our son still sleep. The rooster across the street would greet us, faithfully reminding us that we had made it *before* time. We would lay our child and the other small children on pews, cover them, and begin "calling down heaven."

At some point in the service, I'd continue leading prayer while walking around the room. When I stopped at any given person I would pat them, indicating that they were to retrieve my microphone and take-up the charge. The patted person would pray until they were poured-out, as signaled by the touch of the next intercessor. At the time I thought little about our practice, and it would be years until we all laughed at my *ignorance* and their compliance. We did learn a lot about answered prayer, though.

Reared among the "mourning women of Zion," I grew-up around the altar, attending every form of prayer and praise service. My summers were fun, but part of that fun was meeting the prayer warriors for early morning and noon day prayer. I liked being there. We walked into a dimly lit, quiet place, the antithesis of its normal activities. The only light was courtesy of the beams of color bunching off stained glass.

They'd turn on lights, heat or air, and start singing to signal the transition. Still singing, they'd make their way to the front, anoint themselves with the oil kept beside the altar, and kneel amid moans and groans I now know were signs of aging. Then, the sounds seemed as holy as I saw them. Songs like "Remember Me" or "I Need Thee" entreated the Lord to come see about us. He must have, because the room always changed.

They would begin in unison, thanking and praising God for His manifold benefits. Having entered the gates, thankfully they prayed different things, assured that God could distinguish one request from the other. The start would be slow and steady. Then, one sister would pull out in front, taking the lead, being *led*. The others would come in agreement, acknowledging that she was the one anointed at that moment, like the lead in a singing group.

As if on cue, she would simmer down and another sister would take the reins, as the process worked its way through the flesh and soul, finding its rest when spirit met Spirit. The whole thing fascinated me, partly because I knew something happened every time they called Him. I could not comprehend it then, and can hardly express it now. But the Almighty God, Creator of all, Master of the universe, was interested in hearing from a few stout, sincere, sanctified "sistas" in a small sanctuary in the south. So He'd put His ear to the earth, awaiting their invocation; then He stepped into their world to bring them to His. I couldn't figure out why all my friends weren't interested in this phenomenon. A few were, and I find it noteworthy that they are still intercessors to this day.

Sometimes on bended knees, sometimes laying sideways, sometimes sitting: I slept, listened, and waited my turn, thinking that perhaps something would fall on me. I loved being in "the presence" and although too young to fully appreciate those times, something inside knew it was about another time. The women of our vibrant Virginia church admonished me to "stay close to God and love Him with all your heart, soul, mind, and strength." They encouraged me to talk to Him daily, and assured me that "He will talk back to you." I love them: Alma Williams, Rose Jones, Vance Wright, Gertrude

Gee, Laura Dickerson, and most especially, Grace Conway; for letting me tag along and learn His voice for myself.

My mother and the church mothers were preparing me for a task I didn't know I could do. And now, as a pastor, I was requiring the "Prayers" to do something they didn't know they could do. For intervals of five, ten, then what ended up being fifteen minutes, they were to take the microphone and speak to God in the way they would usually speak, not in old English or like they'd been to seminary.

Through sweat, stammers, and short pauses, they cooperated. No one ever refused the "pat," and I am humbled that they trusted the God in me. I didn't know myself what He was doing in the boot camp we didn't know we had signed up for. The people who faithfully prayed us through those meetings still practice personal prayer time and can be counted on to lead us in prayer whenever or wherever called upon.

Because my husband would later take anyone who came after those days through extensive teaching and training, even our children can lead prayer and volunteer to do so just for fun. I am ever-grateful that prayer for them is not monotonous, strenuous, or laborious. It is a life spent in constant communication with the Dad who is away until He comes to pick us up.

Our praying baby Doves had fun right away in all-night prayer at the church that invited us. With colorful flags and streamers, liturgical praise dancers, and snacks midway, what wasn't to enjoy? The people seemed surprised to see us, initially, but welcomed us once they looked us over. A number of us had come in at once; that may have taken them aback. We were encouraged to spread out and worship with someone we didn't come with.

The pastor was a gentle man who loved God, His people, and His plan. He dreamed of unity within the church and cleaved to the belief that he would witness it. He worshipped with passion, prayed with conviction, and admonished with grace. He was no fraud and wasn't playing games. I believed his greatest desire was to be a bridge that ushered the church from regular service to serious revival. I, too, pray to see that.

So pray we did. From various backgrounds, experiences and

perspectives we gathered, God honoring every attempt. The services were different for us, but we embraced the difference and went whatever direction the River was flowing. We walked, laid, danced, marched, sang, talked, played the tambourine, praised, preached, prophesied and prayed, prayed, and prayed. Our children did likewise, often outlasting most adults, who'd fall asleep shortly after arriving. But I'd hang in there with the youngsters, walking and talking, singing and shouting, but standing mostly because sitting might turn into snoring.

Along with the spiritual benefit was the natural benefit of praying together; we met new people and came to anticipate seeing them each month. God never missed an appointment, but as with most things that don't appeal to our senses, people began to slack off. Eventually, we would end-up with fewer and fewer intercessors, but the few were faithful. Our pastor/friend could be counted on. With the exception of his missions' trips, he'd be present: walking, talking or soaking in God's goodness. He was a man on a mission, and we believed it possible.

I'd like to say we saw it come to pass. I'd like to say we were a part of it. But the vote of 2008 brought about change, and it wasn't democratic, though it may have been demonic in inception. The prayer group was growing weary, but the coalition of color still remained. Even towards the end, there were people of African-American, Caucasian, Latino, and Asian descent lifting up holy hands. Our hands may have been holy, but our hearts still needed work.

One notable night things took a turn. The election of 2008 was in full swing, and ours was a swing state. From seemingly nowhere, a virtual unknown, Barak Hussein Obama, had clinched the presidential nomination and was well on his way to becoming the first man of color in the white house. Just about anyone I knew, of any hue, was astonished or amazed at the prospect. No one was unscathed. The possibility seemed to delight or disturb everyone. You would have been hard-pressed to find neutrality because this was the election of a lifetime and no one seemed uncertain.

Every white person I knew was clear that the man with the middle name like the man who'd attacked our towers was not from God. Each black person I associated with was in concert that "the

Lord had heard the blood of our ancestors crying from the ground and had sent help." Of course, there are those who will tell you that their electoral decision was not as shallow or sensitive as that. But decisions based on high sensitivities often wade in shallow waters.

Such debaters will site statistics, refer to Obama's background, raise the issue of a birth certificate, repeat some line from conservative media, and even rattle the chains of religious folks with prophetic insights of doom and destruction. Opponents will paint a picture of justice for all and equality for any, predict his guidance through economic storms, praise his commitment to end the war, present his academic credentials, and quote the platitudes of some guy name Keith (an MSNBC commentator).

Both sides would speak as political analyst, prolific thinkers, or philosophers, defending the democracy, preserving the republic. They would fight to the end, rally their base, champion their cause. They would make cacophonous claims about the other candidate and stoop to the nadir with election ads. And that was their prerogative as citizens of this country.

My concerns were not as much about the political process as for the church. I saw the body being bruised, fractured, or amputated. And as convenient as it would be to place the blame on a colored man, for this one we must look beyond complexion to the complexities of the human heart. Our hearts had been taken out and lay exposed on the operating table for the world to see.

That election year, I watched friendships dissolve, saw neighbors pretend as if they didn't see me, heard television preachers speak vicious things, believed that any previous strides had been stymied, and prayed our son would not be permanently damaged by any racial statements, suggestions, or signs which reminded him that he was the only African-American boy in his Christian school. I, too, felt my heart was outside of me.

About that time, our son's school asked us to conduct chapel for them. Having done so on many occasions, we accepted. For years the Lord had faithfully inspired our sharing, and I recall each presentation most favorably. A responsibility I always took quite seriously, I went into a time of careful, prayerful consideration. The

Lord always surprised me with what He deemed necessary, and delighted me with the creative way we could do it.

This time was no exception. He gave specific details, and I took copious notes. We were to do a dramatic presentation inspired by the elections of 2008. More importantly, we were to call His body to unity despite those political divides. Chapel was always full, but the special occasion left standing room only. We had planned, practiced, and prayed. Now it was time for "One Body."

The presentation went better than expected. Thunderous laughter filled the room at all the appropriate times. Streams of tears could be seen at others. The mime/dance finale to the popular "I Need You to Survive" was both beautiful and blessed. By the responses that followed, we had fulfilled our assignment. No one has ever stated the obvious, but not everyone wanted to address race and religion in one fair swoop. I have not done chapel there since. Something was not the same.

The members of our church had their own election experiences— co-workers distancing themselves and arguments that escalated into racial divides which almost turned into fist fights. Some members worked with people who have not, to date, acknowledged that a black man ever ran for president, let alone won. For sure, the worst thing to come out of the election that year was the strain to worship together across the apparent colored lines of our city, state, and nation. Pastors will deny that. They have to.

Strangely, our city was especially ripe that election season because it was confronting its own racial divisiveness. An upcoming class on racial reconciliation sparked our curiosity. My husband and I registered, then showed up to see what we had been missing. Years prior, it seemed, groups had been meeting to extricate and disclose an event that was kept secret for one hundred years.

Over dinners, dialogues, and divides, they hashed out their differences and emerged stronger and wiser. The blacks and whites had survived frank talks and faced a tenuous past. When they came up for air, they bore documents, carried plans, and presented their findings to the proper authorities. With that information, they inspired others and ignited the city and state to hear the conclusion of the whole matter. As part of their ongoing effort, the writer of a new novel was in town and scheduled to address the secret of our city's past sin so that the truth could make us free.

His assistant sang of freedom, opening the class with Negro spirituals reminiscent of candle lit church houses in back woods and non-lit tracks supporting the underground railroad. Her voice thundered, starting behind us, then working its way through us. By the time she was finished, we were ready to begin.

The audience was full of all types: political and civic leaders, clergy, educators, business owners, and every day people. The auditorium was in an old locally famous school the speaker had attended as a child. The guest author and activist, preacher's kid and professor, was next. He was Dr. Timothy B. Tyson, an instructor from Duke University. I was interested in what he would say, since he looked rather ordinary. Looks are almost always deceptive. I liked him, immediately, hanging on every word. He was quick-witted, informed, and gifted to interlace information through storytelling. And what stories he had to tell!

Not the least of these had to do with Wilmington, North Carolina, at the end of the 1800s—1898 to be accurate. The political climate was hot. The three popular parties of that time were in a fight to the finish. Tensions ran high and tempers, higher. There was much at stake and both sides knew it. In an attempt to secure the win, a plan was devised to overtake the local government. The first and only successful coup d'e tat in the history of this nation played out in the center of our city!

Because race played a primary role in the violent decision to take back the government, local successful black-owned businesses were destroyed, burned, or taken-over. Families that ran them were run out of town, some hiding in the Cape Fear River or woods. Volatility ensued, pitting neighbor against neighbor and plummeting the city into near ruin. No order was ever issued from the white house, and no one showed up to help. Since the national government looked the other way, no one dared look into the preposterous claims that Wilmington had a secret which needed to be told. Telling it might mean trying to fix it. And who had time for that?

I was floored! Where was I? What in the world had happened here? How could anything good ever grow over such rotten seeds, stained soil, and deceptive foundations? All around were reminders of families that were missing and the ones that replaced them. And then it was the issue of Jim Crow being instituted here before it almost cost our country its soul. I found myself wrestling with those realities and the reason God would want *me* here. Fighting sexism was already an uphill battle, so fighting racism was nothing I looked forward to sparring. I endured enough skirmishes being reared in the back yard of civil war grounds.

The mixed-multitude of men and women who had met for years to bring this situation to light was courageous, audacious, and relentless. They had lived with the residuals of racial rifts and been haunted by the stories their grandparents told them *not* to tell. Who would believe them anyway? The world had marked them as liars and losers, but they would win. Out of those racial reconciliation meetings they were in the process of healing; now, together, they would be heard, and others would take up their charge and echo their cry.

Shortly after that class, we stood in the chambers of city council and heard the government officially acknowledge what happened in 1898, apologizing for its inactivity and insensitivity. While there, a wonderful wave washed over me because I remembered that Descending Dove had recently used the space and took the liberty of praying over this room and each seat of those who govern from here. Maybe that is one reason I have been called to this city.

I was proud of Wilmington for endeavoring to do better. I am fond of the people who faced off to fight injustice. I have seen the promise land, and *it is here*. It's beginning to feel more like home. Though the city seemed willing to try, the church community seemed less sure. In example, the night the "lights" went out in Wilmington.

Service was well underway in our all night prayer meeting. At another location, the room was almost packed when we arrived. Enthusiasm filled the air, and after smiles, handshakes, and head nods, we started. Thanksgiving and praise and worship were welcoming, inviting all to enter in. Now through the gates, we received the pastor's official greeting and encouraged the visitor who responded. Then it was time to get down to business. We were here to pray, and I believed we were more desperate than at any previous gathering.

The agenda that night included the elections, a topic I knew we needed to tackle. It had been an albatross about the necks of many, so I looked forward to collectively attacking it. Surely our group could handle the assignment: surely we could alter the course of our churches and community and take back our city. Certainly we would be used by God to release His will and decree His heart. But *ours* may have gotten in the way.

While seated in anticipation, hands raised, head back, and eyes closed, I thought I heard my name, then my spouse's. We were being called upon to lead the next prayer item. As we walked forward, the power point changed to reveal our topic: the Election of 2008. I had wanted *someone* to pray, for this was the topic that seemed to hold our country captive. I wanted to remain seated. I felt the onus of that moment, but was determined to talk to God until He talked back.

Before we began, the instructions were made clear, and that clarification changed my posture. My husband and I were called on to pray the way *we* wanted the vote to go. By "we," I mean the majority of people present. We all were expected to pray for presidential and vice-presidential candidates John McCain and Sarah Palin: their families, campaign, victory, etc. Although instructions were not given by the pastor who had originally invited us to these meetings, it was the prevailing belief in the room and we were to come in agreement. Someone had assumed that all Christians were voting Republican and would later state that "anyone who didn't, didn't love Jesus." People I knew and loved did love Jesus. Many of them were voting Democratic—some for the first time in their lives.

So that night, I could not comply. For me, it wasn't that cut and dry. I was in a quandary, had been for months. I followed each debate, read multiple articles, listened to various broadcasts, weighed both sides' arguments, conferred with friends, chided with family, and requested divine direction to decide. All around us people became besotted with their party. My family seemed to be the only one outside the obvious. That's why we came to prayer...to ask.

Race seemed to cloud all judgment, but everyone called it "God," and kept it moving. I didn't want to do that, so I paused. Looking about the room, I apologized for not going forth, requesting prayer myself. It would not be godly, to me, to pray for one party, and not ask Him to bless, help, and keep *both*. Nor could I pray from a vantage point of His favor applying to what *I* liked only. Prayer is seeking and speaking His will, not mine. And I so wanted to know what part I was to play.

Standing united, my husband and I joined hands and invoked Father God. Some agreed, some resented, and some remained silent. Those present seemed to pray without much heart to me. It was still on the spiritual operating table waiting to be made new. But if left outside the body too long, one's time could *expire*. It did. We made other prayer meetings, but the air was still "heavy" with something none of us dare mention. Not long after that election prayer, we excused ourselves. Possibly, we will return one day, after we have been under His knife, and *all* our hearts are pumping His blood.

Election night, finally, came. I stood in front of the television awaiting results. Barak Obama was now the first African-American president of the United States of America. Turning off lights that night I noticed an odd sight. None of our neighbors had *any* lights on. With the exception of street lights, our community was black. I wondered was it like that all over?

All night prayer was the only light in our city at that time. Others had flickered and faded. A practice of the Wilmington Race Riot Commission could help us; after we sing "Let Us Break Bread, Together," perhaps we *should* break bread together. Before we gather at the communion table, maybe we should sit at each other's table. Pass the bread, please!

CHAPTER 14

The Pain of Parting

THIS IS THE stuff no pastor wants to say. It is much more comfortable sharing success stories and statistical data about the size of our congregations. We'd rather speak of what makes us look good than reveal the part of this position that pains us the most. No pastor is immune to it, but most will act as if they took a pill, and it went away. This is the chapter I didn't want to write, but knew I must so that the virus can be treated effectively.

You see a lot in an airport.

There is the consistent ebb and flow of those arriving or departing. Before we were attacked and our airports under siege, you could go as far as the gate to see someone off. That was the scene which pulled my heart strings the most. Chocolate being passed off to the son in fatigues, flowers smashed in grandma's hand to remind her of the holiday that hurled by, squeezes to the sister about to start her freshman year, and mom's lipstick on the face of the new missions student.

They were departing, and the pain was piercing. One ache had to do with their safety: the other, the separation. As the plane taxied the runway, then became smaller with altitude, loved ones stood too close to the window, waving, mouthing something, as if they could be seen or heard. They would call them back, if they could. But as soon as they'd purchased the ticket... they were already gone.

All pastors know the pain of parting. We have sat across the desk listening to countless stories of how God was calling them away from the ministry, how their season had changed, and how much they appreciated all the Lord had used us to do. But the final line read the same way, "*We out!*"

At the request for the meeting, you often knew what it was about because they had never required an audience before. You tried to avoid the urge to dissuade them to go or persuade them to settle down and get an answer in peace. But you already spoke more than you wanted to. They almost always seemed restless, anxious, out-of-sorts, as if they had a plane to catch. My pastor told me that if people ever want to leave, do not slow them down or stop them; you will only prolong the inevitable. And later is often more dramatic and traumatic—for everyone.

From the very beginning I dealt with a mass exodus, which had less to do with me than their loyalty to the old pastor. Some were just freaked out by a female with a fresh word to share every Sunday. I got that. It was the ones who committed to stay and help rebuild that I took issue with. The first to go after I was installed as pastor was an unlikely pair.

We didn't know them as well because they came in spurts, but they were kind, and we shared a casual, cordial relationship. I personally liked them and could see how God might use them when they grew a little. Apparently, they weren't growing at a pace they liked. They "called a meeting." In the cramped quarters of my light-less office they began with "Thank you," then transitioned. I had a Charlie Brown moment, unsure of anything that followed, "We just want more!" *Ouch!* I thought. *Why so low beneath the belt?*

That one statement could have marred me because it was finger-pointedly personal. If there wasn't enough sustenance, wasn't *I* responsible, since I was the one in the kitchen? Going further, they spoke of a newly formed ministry, and how their visit provided "so much more" than what we had. There is was again, that *pinch* in the pit of my gut.

I sat stupefied for a few seconds, and then thanked them for at least saying good-bye. We shook hands, and they strolled down the middle aisle, free to explore "more." Relaying their resignation to leaders later, I was given additional information that granted lucidity. A joke referencing their baby had been heard by them and elicited fiery indignation. In short, they were hurt and offended by someone they perceived as close to me. That was my first *ah-ha* moment. I reprimanded the people who had been so insensitive, but gained valuable insight for the remainder of my pastorate.

People do not just leave their church, and rarely is God sending them away. Something happens. Some situation, spiritual sibling rivalry, or sore spot ignites the flame of offense. It wares numerous disguises and seldom shows up as itself, but *offense* is its name and if not lanced, it can be infectious. It takes various forms, but the results are the same. Below are the offended I've encounter over the years:

The Hopper—this is the person who is ever-visiting. They make no promises, give no significant offering, and will not remain. Having passed-through three churches in the past five years, they make no allegiance to any assembly. They are transient, gypsies, or often, orphans. Some have lived through pastoral rejection, neglect, or abandonment. Most have personal stories of parent-child traumas and are suspicious by necessity. They have seldom received a father's blessing because trust is broken. They smile and sway, but they will not surrender easily. And they will not stay-put long enough to heal.

The Invisible—these are those who were so excited to finally take the right hand of fellowship. They had come from another place and looked forward to using their talents, skills, and abilities to further the vision. But one Sunday, *they* were not visible. You asked around, but no one had seen or heard from them. Bible Study came and went, but there was no word. The next Sunday repeated the first. Attempts were made to call, but to no avail. Messages were left unanswered. They seemed to have disappeared, vanished without a trace. When you finally made contact, by mistake, they would only reveal that they "will not be returning." You would not see them again, and you are left to make suppositions while sifting through the ruins that remain.

The Deep—this kind is not offended, angry, or hurt, though they are no longer smiling. They hold no ill-will and have no complaints to speak of. They have just emerged from their prayer closets, latest conference, or prophecy session to announce what they "received." Deep had called unto deep, and they sensed the need to go *deeper*. Nothing you or anyone else in the ministry said had ever fed them, freed them, or fascinated them in the way this recent encounter had. And they must follow "the leading." They were way too enraptured to hear anything you had to say, since the Lord had bypassed you to speak directly to them. The purpose of their courtesy was to "do the right thing," not request advice, prayer, or release. As their *former* pastor, you were not called to speak—they were. There was so much more to be done, so much more to say. But that's just the thing, they were done *hearing*. And although you were once the voice God used to help them, they were no longer interested in your help.

The Protestor—they refuse to leave right away, though obviously dissatisfied with something. They are faithful to a fault, arriving before time, leaving when the parking lot lights are turned off. They may not have been the life of the party, but now, for whatever reason, they are lifeless. They participate, but barely. They sit, often in silence, when anyone who they don't agree with is active. They don't mind bringing glory to themselves, and they have a point to make. "Somebody Done Somebody Wrong" becomes their theme song. It may not even be to them, but they have a point to prove. Since it may be too "out-of-order" to say it, they'll just show it. In their folded hands is a sign of offense for all the church to see. They will leave one day, but not before at least one other person knows why.

The Love Said So—this type is generally sweet, sound, supportive. Sometimes new, they are almost always spiritually stunted in some way. They are quiet for the most part, but do revel in company and don't like being alone. Soft spoken, they will not shout you down while you are preaching, but they will try to live by the tenants of the sacred text—with one notable exception: love and relationship is where you part ways. These are those who assert that a *schizophrenic god* told them to both marry and divorce the *same* person. They love you, so they are not as offended with you as with the word "Wait!" They *have been waiting*! Now love has come at last, and they must follow their heart—the one that is "deceitful above all things and desperately wicked." You do love them and want them to be "in love." You only urge them to look both ways before they cross the street or hold your hand while doing so. But they will not heed; they are already breaking away, making a mad dash to the altar or city hall. The wedding was planned long before you were privy: you were just on the guest list. Now, you have been the party pooper and they are parting.

The Assigned—they were wounded years ago by something you said or didn't say, did or didn't do. Since then, insult has been added to injury, but nothing was ever said, so you think all is well.

You don't know what you or anyone else did, but they relive it as if it happened, yesterday. Every time you do something that reminds them of your initial misstep, they grow more disappointed. They like the ministry, though, so they are never leaving—not physically. But they are never again fully engaged. They are on assignment. What starts out as a personal problem becomes demonically infected, if left to fester. They will frustrate, debate, and try to castrate other parts of the body. But they intend to stay.

The Iscariot—this is the sort the Bible warned you about. The one who ate at your table, slept in your space, and smiled in your face while harboring a fugitive. Some like you *too* much, wanting you to themselves. Some want to be like you, created in *your image*. Some just like being in your space so others will see them as "close." Though near, they never really make connection. They don't mind carrying your money bag...I mean, briefcase. They may handle your business. They may buy you things. But they are just buying time because there is a hole in their heart. They may not even know it exists, but when you are honored by a woman with an alabaster box, they will see it as waste. They would have done it another way. Satan sees the opening, and he will wait. The day you stop teaching the multitudes to teach them, they resent it. They nod in approval, but their heart is not in agreement. The hole widens. They may sit at your table, but they have turned on you.

Any of the above could cross lines or combine, but they have the same commonality: they are offended. I wanted to include a case that ended decently and in order, but I have not yet lived through one. I am the kind of pastor who looks forward to sending someone out with the blessing. For that, I will have to hold fast.

People perceive their pastor to be whoever or whatever they want or need: parent, child, buddy, therapist, personal trainer, life coach, loan-officer, prayer-partner, savior: all distorted images. When any of the silent expectations go unmet, people get sad, upset, irritated—offended. This is not what they signed up for: you are not who they expected. They want out because it is their way of telling you that the relationship has taken a turn for the worst. Telling you what hurts might seem too petty, staying might seem too painful. Exiting is easier.

I wanted to exit once. My pastor and I had a serious disagreement. I didn't like her then and am sure she could have done without me. But there we were, locked in a battle of wills (*hers, mine, and His*). Her attempts to correct me had cut me deeply, since no one had ever made such insinuations. In addition, I felt she was being abrasive and absurd in her advice. I was fairly new to the ministry, via my husband, and could not possibly conceive of how she thought to "read me." In my opinion, a minor infraction had spun out of control and she was getting on my nerves. So my season had to be up, right?"

Were it not for the wisdom of my wonderful praying husband and his refusal to run, this story would have abruptly ended. But there is so much more to tell. She and I would continue to meet. I sat through grueling classes that seemed to target me. I returned home many nights, in tears, because I felt I was being misunderstood and mistreated. I could not imagine how God's will was wrapped up in my waiting. *Why couldn't we just begin again somewhere else?* One reason—because I could not outrun myself. The other—the time you want to run the most is the worst time to do so. That is not what she said; it is what God unveiled to me as we made ourselves keep going to church.

In addition, one night in a dream, the Lord paraded a line of leaders in my life, beginning with my father. I jumped out of bed to take notes since the scenes were so vivid. When there were no more names to write, I scanned the list to make sure I had gotten them all. Then, I saw the connection: I felt they had each failed me in some way, though I served them faithfully. Most certainly I would hold any other leader hostage. I was suspect and shrouded. I repented and asked my pastor's pardon.

I do not condone pastoral abuse in any form, seeing that as abnormal use of the position. But I am confident that olives must be crushed before there is oil; grapes smashed before there is wine. God sometimes uses the pastoral office to apply just enough pressure to break our flesh. Our spirits should remain intact, and our "juices" flowing. Even ungodly Penninahs make Hagars (the two wives whose rivalry led to the barren woman bearing a child [1 Sam. 1]) "push."

We survived the test: my pastor, my husband, and I. What we had no way of knowing is that it was the final exam before graduation. The call to pastor would soon follow, but not before we had passed. In the months and years that followed, we would rely heavily on each other because only we understood the lessons of the class we had taken together. The subject: Offense 101. Since then, I have seen many people fail that class, and they have repeated it over and over again. To compensate, they work harder than they should to prove that they are, in fact, sent. You do not have to complete it with honors, but promotion comes only after you pass the Offense class.

I am not so stringent as to suggest that everyone is for every church. I John 2:19 bares that out: "They went out from us, but they were not of us; for if they had been of us, they would no doubt have continued with us: but they went out that they might be made manifest that they were not of us."

That being stated, the scripture is, however, clear that there is a place of your blessing, an assigned place. There, we are developed and matured. We understood that, which is why we joined in the first place. The Word and the way it was presented, the people, and the place—all spoke to *who* we were and *what* we were called to do. It was not the perfect place, full of imperfect people, but we knew we fit. So we heeded the call for discipleship and committed to the cause. Or did we? Perhaps there were ulterior motives, other agendas, or ladders to climb.

In the generation of instantaneous, you would be hard-pressed to find anyone who lives in the same house, works at the same job, or is married to the same person they were twenty, even ten, years ago. Ours is an ever-changing culture. Long gone is the telephone number you had as a child and still remember, the couple you could count on to give you marital counsel, or the car you'd driven until it was paid off. Because the church lives alongside the world, our commitments, too, are short lived. So where we worship becomes like anything else: our dedication to it as long as the latest fashion trend. Like anything else we are able to change—mates, shoes, hairdos—we see church as something to be discarded when it does not suit us or fit our plans any longer.

From Antioch through the epistles, church participants seemed to remain steady. Perhaps the lack of choices prevented them from hopping or swapping. New ministries are popping up daily, the latest sometimes "borrowing" members from other churches. People have left our church to attend other churches, whose members left to attend our church. The revolving door is not only broken, it is useless. No one is added to the kingdom when we are merely trading places.

People depart for all kinds of reasons: career changes, military transfers, matrimony, academia, loss of a loved one, or because they were "sent." Every pastor should know that. But there is a biblical order for "going out." *How* one leaves should be as much God as how they came. Something should be said, understood, agreed upon. If pastors are a gift from God to help build-up and grow-up His People, according to Ephesians 4:11–12, they should have space to share. What my pastor shared at the time I was offended was confirmed by God years later. It brought me to tearful introspection. I had not known that about myself and am sure she could *only* have known it by divine "download." I often wince at the idea that I almost moved out of place, time, and turn. If I had followed my offense, I would have forfeited the blessings I am basking in. My pastor recently taught us a brief lesson. Using the verse of scripture relating to Jesus going to synagogue, as was His custom, she asked the rhetorical question, "What in the world could they have taught Jesus in synagogue that He, as God, didn't already know?" She offered the answer, "Nothing! He wasn't there for what He could *get*, but what He could *give*." Perhaps, that should be our custom.

Pastors are not what people have projected onto them. We bend, break, and sometimes bleed. When people depart, pastors feel betrayed: the covenant has been breached. I know. One lives inside me. We don't get it *all* right. Sometimes we get it *all* wrong. But we have been vetted to cast a vision and see it to the finish. In a church, we are the only ones who have to stay, but we cannot complete kingdom mandates alone. Someone must see it through, stay until the curtain-call, "endure hardness as a good soldier (2 Tim. 2:3)," finish well. If the time should ever come that you must part, please try not to slam the door on your way out. It makes the whole house shake...and pastors ache.

CHAPTER 15

Amazing Grace

I GREW UP WITH Grace. She is my mother. Dark brown sugar-skinned with a broad smile, she was reared down south and a force to be reckoned with. Her southern heritage came with its own reward. She cleans house like a profession, not just straightening up either—washing baseboards, stripping floors, getting cobwebs out the corners. There is an order to her cleaning; glasses are washed *before* dishes and utensils (so the grease won't set on them), and you're not done until you fold *and* put away the clothes you washed. The smell of Clorox meets visitors at our front door, and her bathrooms smell like Pine Sol. Saturdays are cleaning days, so no one enjoys the comfort of sleeping in.

She cooks better than most chefs: smothering pork chops, deep frying golden moist chicken, lacing eggs with extra sharp cheddar, and baptizing yams in nutmeg and vanilla extract. The top layer of her macaroni and cheese is orange and her sweet potato pie, deep rust. A pig doesn't stand a chance in her kitchen because she can find use for all of it, snout to tail. She makes most people repent for saying they loathe liver and onions. A pot of her black-eyed peas with smoked neck bones, okra, and sweet stewed tomatoes would go far on frigid Virginia nights. The scent of her baked goods beckons residents and neighbors to "Come, get yo' blessing." Many do. Her door is always open because she never meets a stranger.

Around her table there are laughs abundant. She is hilarious without trying, commanding the attention of her greedy guests. She is an adroit story teller, painting scenes her audience can see. She is witty and wise, throwing out lines before we can recuperate from the last one, and catching jokes before others might.

Highly intelligent, she was offered scholarships she didn't take because mothering was something you had to be present to do. She fills out friend's forms and speaks for those who can't articulate their position. She writes legal letters to get people their due, many of which are admired by attorneys representing the *other* side.

Together, she and her activist friends fight like girls, winning victories for the least, last, and lost. They ran the housing projects we once lived in, and everyone knew it.

A single mom, she is not disillusioned by the idea that she can be *both* mother and father. She believes there are things a father brings to the table that no mother can. For that, we would have to accept God as Father and let Him make up the difference. She is committed to being the best mother she can be, "leaning on His everlasting arm."

Once she shared the story of how we got to the church that would shape our lives.

Determined *that* Sunday to find us a church home, she dressed me and my young brother and started walking the streets of our city. We didn't have a car, so she stopped often to see how we were faring, or swept my brother up in her arms to placate his restlessness. On Harding Street, we came upon Bethesda. Though we had passed other houses of worship, it was this one, she said, that caught *my* attention. Pointing and proclaiming "This is the one, Ma," we stepped inside. I would not step outside until I was going away to college.

My mother would go on to grow in grace: directing choir, dancing a "mean holy gig," writing dramas, teaching, preaching (aka, testifying or emceeing), counseling, interceding, leading multitudes to Christ, and helping with water and Holy Spirit baptism. Her church bestowed the honorable title of church "Mother" upon her. She had been that all along. Mama needs no cajoling to do what her position requires. Her pastor and his wife love her. The church adores her. She has not given him any trouble, and she would not do anything to lead them away from God. He is her life, her hope, her *everything*. Everyone knows it.

The mother of invention, she can make something out of nothing. Because we grew up without a father's finances, she had to learn to stretch *change*, not just dollars. She turned flour into the best homemade biscuits, made any beans a meal, kept kerosene lamps (in case the lights were turned off), and filled the bathtub with water when she knew the bill was passed due.

Growing up, we sometimes lived from pillar to post, mainly with relatives who were not happy to see *all* of us coming to spend the night. We've been separated as siblings, slept in rooms over brothels, and seen our furniture on the side of the street. But you wouldn't have known that by her deportment and demeanor. She sang or hummed a lot, smiled in spite of, and assured us that all we had to do was "keep living." I have only seen her cry once. When she did, I hadn't a clue how to respond, so I rubbed her back. She regained her composure and went on about her business. I pondered what could have made her so strong, and wondered if she'd like being weak for a while.

The best listener, you can say anything to her without fear of hearing it repeated. She is non-judgmental, seeing all flesh as flawed, so never showing shock at what sin produces in all people. She is quick to hear and slow to speak in matters of life and love. Prayerfully receiving, she gives only what she believes will help. Our friends enjoy her company and counsel so much that they visit even when we're not home.

One friend showed up at her door in the middle of the night because his own family disowned him. He was, you see, gay. I didn't even understand the term at the time of this incident, but I knew he had done something so repulsive that his own parents could not bear to look upon him. Having survived the abuse of someone he trusted, he had practiced a homosexual lifestyle in secret. Tonight, he had shown up at our house dressed *as a woman*.

I knew he was "funny;" I had heard my siblings laugh at that many times. But this night no one was laughing. He was sobbing. My mother covered him with something and walked him into her kitchen, her office. There she whipped up a quick meal, brewed coffee, and just listened. Sneaking to peek, I wondered what our church members would say if they could see what I saw. My mother didn't care because she was a mother *first*, and he had lost one. I eventually retired, because the empty coffee pot suggested that they were in it for the long haul. The next morning would find me sharing my breakfast and bathroom with our gay guest.

That was one night of my childhood. I am unsure of how long he stayed, but I knew he would always be welcomed back because I know her. After he left, he would keep his promise to keep in touch. Over the years mama would mention speaking to him on occasions, but I was not sure if she had seen him. I did.

I was grown, married, a mother myself. This clean-cut, slender, well-suited white gentleman approached me after a service. Something in his voice was familiar, but I could not recall it before he revealed his identity. He was the gay guy who shared our home and hearts. As soon as we were freed from our embrace, he introduced me to his wife and children. To give her clarity he added, "This is the daughter of the lady I always told you about, Ms. Grace. That lady saved my life!" Standing there, I learned that *God* had, in truth, saved him, but salvation came *by Grace*.

Gifted and talented, she can draw, write, and act. Her acting would get me out of a hard place. I was directing a drama in Williamsburg, Virginia. One of the main characters informed me that an emergency would prevent her participation. I understood her crisis, but the news created one for me. There was no understudy for her role. I put in a frantic call to my mother, who agreed to help me. Over the telephone we discussed the gist of the part, then prayed.

She was in town within hours, but had less than hours to learn lines. Instead, she opted to learn what she could, as sound checks were underway, and adlib the rest. Ad-libbing, I thought, was good for singing the lead in a gospel song, but not for the main role in a drama. I was nail-biting nervous. But she donned her costume, closed her eyes for make-up, then sat meditating in a chair. I was pacing, pensive. The noise from the seats out front signaled the need to get in place. Since I, too, had a small role to play, I didn't know how I would survive the show. But it was a show, so it had to go on.

The curtains rose on cue and the first act was about to begin. Performed in a small theater to a crowd that was just enough to be encouraging, I eased. Things were going well, but my mother's part was forthcoming. She entered stage right, projecting her opening lines. They went over well, but she had plenty more where that came from. As if plugged in, she felt the role, making up her own lines, taking control of her character. She provided just enough memorized lead-ins to cue the next actor, but owned her part like the consummate professional. She acted, sang the old hymn the part required, and danced like the old woman she portrayed. The audience couldn't get enough. They loved her, laughing when she cut up, crying when her character died.

I cried, too, *out of control*. But this was not a drama, this was my mama. The call came when the worst ones do, in the predawn hours. My mother had been diagnosed with cancer shortly after I became a pastor. The news was distressing, but we were hopeful of the new treatment the Richmond, Virginia, specialist wanted to try. While she underwent chemo and radiation, I was told to stay and "help heal the people." She and I spoke daily, usually, throughout the day. She never sounded unlike herself, but we would pop in periodically to make sure. On one visit, she was so ecstatic to see us that she sat in the same chair most of that day, laughing, offering us food, and playing with the baby. He had learned to walk there, so seeing him roam about tickled her. That evening we watched a movie we heard was good, *The Shawshank Redemption*. It was gritty and grimy, but redemption in any movie is a theme I esteem. I have not seen it since.

The time flew by too fast, so we prepared to depart. We kissed her forehead, grabbed the gift she insisted we take, and loaded the van. Closing doors, we heard her constant closing remark, "Love one another." Releasing our love, we waved, blew kisses, and rolled away. Then, my mother did something so uncharacteristic of herself, it is etched in my memory. As we rounded the bend where she lived, I looked back toward her house for some strange reason. She had made it from the front door to a back window, *quickly*, and was smiling, waving, and blowing kisses. She had never done that, and I didn't know why she did then.

The early morning call came from my brother-in-law who told me to "Pray, because it didn't look good." Lifting my head, I shook my husband and summoned a sister from our church to call *anyone* who would pray. Before I could crawl out of bed or gain my composure, the second call came, and it was *not* good...for me. Grace had gone to glory.

My knees buckled under me; I could not hold myself upright. My husband could not console me because this was his other mother, and the pain was as great. He moved about wailing, panting, mourning. When we could, we called our pastor, who cried herself, then helped me pull it together; there was work to be done. I didn't *want* to work, think, or move. I wanted my friend, confidante, teacher, prayer partner, "road dog," supporter, trainer, house keeper, cook, writer, cut up, listener, actor, activist, artist, advocate...mother.

Our family packed in a hurry and drove the long interstate 95 in virtual silence. When we spoke, it was through cracked voices and watered eyes. I knew my husband endeavored to bear me, but we both had to be carried. I cannot summon a memory of our drive, but I knew the city of my rearing would never resemble itself again.

Arriving at my mother's in the middle of the afternoon, everything about that day seemed bleak. With the key she had given, we let ourselves in. Inside was surreal. The home that had served as a refuge for many and therapist's office for any was groaning. There were no food smells, familiar giggles, or friendly welcome. There was just grief. The always bustling domicile was dying. I went from room to room in utter bemusement, crying, shaking my head, disbelieving.

We had spoken the day before, and she assured me that all was well. I sat on the bed she and I shared many times. She once commented that I was "the biggest child she knew who still slept with her mama." I did; every time I was home from college, I'd climb right beside her until her backside warmed mine. Because the men and women of her generation were not "mushy," I knew this was her way of allowing affection. We wouldn't enjoy the moment long because she always worked the graveyard shift and needed to leave soon after I'd claim my spot beside her.

Greetings downstairs informed me that company was here. A steady stream poured in. From that moment on, the family, friends, food, and funeral home would prevail. Out of necessity, the first family to arrive would have to make arrangements. The funeral home had a schedule, and my mother didn't have a will, a fact I found hard to fathom since she helped others with their personal affairs. It could have been that my mother was among those who considered writing a will as inviting death, so they avoid doing so to signal death to stay away. The avoidance would come at a high cost and have residual impact.

My mother's "Home Going" was the kind she'd have liked. Through a historic snow storm, people still came from near and far to say their formal farewells. The service was held at Mt. Olivet Baptist, our city's largest, newest church, courtesy of the pastor, a personal friend. The songs were her "speed," speaking of heaven and telling folks how to get there. The Arts ministry of our church, which she loved, paid tribute with "When Sunday Comes."

We celebrated her contributions, commemorated her part in our plights, and then committed her body to the ground. We shook hands, received cards, accepted condolences, ate, took what remained, and returned to our "regularly scheduled programs," as if this had been a crude commercial. But life had been sucked out and like a lone child, I wanted my mama and could not see days ahead *without her*. A "chance" encounter would provide the mouth-to-mouth I needed to live again.

I rested in the guest room at Greater Grace Temple in Detroit, Michigan. Between sessions I looked over the program, discovering that the evening speaker was someone from my childhood. I looked up to her even then because she was everything other women were not. She was tall and stately, like her family, commanding a room upon entry. In addition, she could sing, direct, and play the organ to shame any man. She, too, was one of those "boot-leg" preachers who always had something profound to say. She could preach as well as most male preachers I knew, in style and substance. She would, eventually, find her own voice and except her own call.

Tonight, this spiritual icon was a few feet away from me, in another room, preparing to minister. I asked her adjutant to allow me to speak to her before we were both too busy. Entering her room, she stood up to express surprise at seeing me after all these years. We were left alone to "catch up." I felt so special, sitting before one of my "sheroes" and not having her belittle what I was there to do. She was the *special* guest, I, the opening act, so to speak. She may have endured so much discrimination that she refused to disparage the ones she had paved the road for.

Determined not to take up too much of her time, I began to excuse myself. While rising, she asked about "Mother Grace." When I told her my mother had passed months prior, she questioned why I was in Detroit. She strongly urged me to "take some time to grieve," explaining the danger of "business as usual." I had not considered that, thinking that plowing ahead would relieve the agony in my heart. I left Detroit fully intending to heed her advice...when I had time to do so.

I was made to. The Sunday following my mother's funeral, I was in the pulpit. I had even returned days before to rehearse with the Arts ministry and ensure everyone was well. They had the honor of meeting and loving my mother and were deeply saddened for me. Mere months had transpired since her passing, and I was busy as a queen bee.

Everything I did as a preacher, back then, took all day. Still a new wife, new mother, and now, new pastor, even preparing messages left sparse room for anything else. Saturdays were basically shut-ins. Sundays were marathons: Sunday school, prayer before service, worship service, meetings, dinner-on-the-go, the drive back to our city, putting the baby down, changing clothes, driving back to church, evening service, more meetings, and driving back home. So I was not impervious to pain, I just didn't have room on my plate for it.

Because it was Monday, I took this day "off" to order my house. In the kitchen I craved milk and went about retrieving a glass. After pouring it, I set it on the counter and continued doing something else. When I went to reach for it, the glass slipped just shy of my grasp, landing on the floor. On the other side of the counter I saw the milky mess. Before I could pick up all the pieces, I let out a scream. Shocking myself, I began to cry out loud. *What was happening? Was I going mad? What had I missed?* Everything about the moment was confounding. Then, the words of that well-known preacher lady spoke back to me: "If you don't let yourself grieve, it will come upon you out of nowhere. I know, Angel. I lost my mom, too."

I was not crying over spilled milk, but the broken glass mirrored my broken heart: the one I had not given a proper place to grieve. It was making its own space. I fell across my sofa, at first on bended knees, and then flat on my back staring at a lofty ceiling. Somewhere past that roof, sky, vast expanse, was my mother. She had moved in with Jesus, and left no forwarding address. I did not feel like a pastor or a saint. I was in anguish and more angry than I dare admit. But God already knew that. I yelled at Him, cried out to Him, questioned Him. And, much to His credit and my amazement, He let me. He did not rebuke, restrain, or revile me. He just heard me out, like He did Job. I saw another side of Dad that day.

When I was done, I lay sullen and soaked. It was God's turn to speak, answering my accusation. "You took her! You took my mama!" I had yelped.

To which He responded, "Yes, I did. I took her."

My reply, "That's what I said, so I don't get it?"

"I did. *Me*, Angel! Not the enemy, a stranger, or the grim reaper. Your mother belonged to Me. I put *My hands* under her weary frame and brought her to Me."

I knew, at once, that no enemy had had access to her. No demon had despoiled her body. My mother was not just well, but all well! She had spent her final moments on this side working out the details of her own departure. She knew we would not be alone. The Comforter had comforted *her* and would have to do the same for everyone whose pain was pulling them apart.

That truth began to pull the pieces of my heart together. We continued our conversation without condemnation. To the point of my wanting her to see my new car; I was assured that she would know. My desire to have her abandon newly tread *golden* streets to ride in my Lexus on asphalt became increasingly unreasonable. Before we ended, He set my heart at ease by affording me the privilege of telling Him anything I wanted forwarded. I comprehended our agreement, since Scripture is not silent about attempts to converse with the deceased. I'm unsure of when I fell asleep, but I awakened renewed. After that day, I would cry when I touched anything connected to her, get choked up at the mention of her name, and miss her *dearly*. But the gift of grief granted me relief, applying ointment where I needed it most. Time does *not* heal all things, but time with Him can heal *us*.

I was honored to have the pleasure of my mother's company when I preached. She would intercede, speak her support, and stand in approval of what God called me to do. There was no flattering or stroking the ego. Her only compliment was always the same, "The

Lord really used you today, Baby!" That being interpreted: "Don't ever think you can do this without Him." I still can't!

Mama made her way to our church whenever she could and helped herself every time she did. On one of her last visits, she taught me a life lesson. Our toddler was glad service had ended, so he could finally cavort with his cousins. They were little people like him. Since most Sundays ushered in visitors, I shook hands and spoke to the people my husband missed. My mother made her rounds, too, providing encouragement to anyone who didn't want to burden the pastor, but had a problem.

Our son waltzed through legs and made his way to my skirt. "Mommy, Mommy!" he pulled, "Mommy!"

"Excuse me," I said, extending courtesy to our company. "Wait a minute, son. Mommy's talking."

"But Mommy, Mommy...," he insisted to the point of irritation. Giving him "the look," he closed his mouth, but wasn't satisfied.

Watching the scene play out from across the sanctuary, my mother moved in my direction. Without interrupting my conversation she stood beside me facing the opposite direction. She took my hand to signal she was ready to speak, then whispered, "Your son is trying to speak to you." I already knew that; that's why he was standing there looking unhappy. She repeated, "*Your* son is trying to speak to *you*." Having reiterated, she moved away, assured that I would translate the meaning. What she really meant was, "You are called to this child and his father first; all others will have to always line up at the back door."

I informed the person vying for my attention that my son wanted me, and he was a *very special* little boy. I do not recall what he said that day, that's how childish it was, but I do remember the look on his face when he realized that he had been moved to the front of the line, and *always* had my permission to break through. What I granted him that day was *grace*. He would never again have to earn, beg, or work for my attention. He could have it just because he is *my son*. Her lesson made me a better parent, not just a better pastor.

I am a grace preacher. Not because we are excused to live loosely or like the world we are called to "light;" but because our church needed lots of it, and it has borne us on Dove wings. It has saved us, sustained us, and overshadowed us while we journeyed. By the time I accepted this assignment, it was already clear that living by law was an impossible task. For years, the people I shepherded endeavored to follow the strict guidelines they assumed could save them, only to fall short every time. What they needed was not more policy and procedure, but a way of escape, a way to be free—grace that was greater than *all our sins*.

What is amazing about grace is that it provides what you don't deserve while holding back what you do. We have failed, miserably, grown frustrated, and are flawed, terribly. But it is "not of ourselves: less any man should boast." Since we reside on "Grace Street," there is never anything to brag about: everywhere we've been—God took us; anything we are—God made us; and everything we have—God gave us. Once He gave us a woman named Grace, and she was truly amazing.

> Amazing grace, how sweet the sound
> That saved a wretch like me
> I once was lost, but now I'm found
> Was blind, but now I see
>
> Through many dangers, toils, and snares
> I have already come;
> 'Tis grace hath brought me safe thus far
> And grace will lead me home.

—By John Newton

Child's Play

CHILDREN TEACH US many things, not the least of which is how God sees us—as children, not His little adults. We are ever growing, but will never out grow Him. I have gleaned more lessons about Father God from our son than all the information in many books combined. I am fully persuaded that living with him has granted me inestimable ministry material. Loving him has transformed my thinking, behavior, and pastorate. He has captured my heart, and many people have been the recipients of the love *he* showed *me*. I am a gentler, kinder, more tender soul after dealing with him. I may be the teacher, but in many instances, I have been *his* student. I may owe him money (smirk).

He hasn't done enough of the normal kid stuff to create a good comedy skit or warrant a ride in the ambulance: he never put pennies up his nose, wrapped himself in toilet paper, drank bleach, or blew up the microwave. He *did* completely cover himself with petroleum jelly, eating a bit, and chased a basketball across the fellowship hall floor during my installation as pastor. For the former, I faulted myself for leaving the tempting concoction on the counter, and for the latter, I faulted the individual who took the ball out of the van and gave it to him (his dad).

He is smooth, strong, studious, and stable. No longer shy, he is reserved and will not fake funny. He smiles often, but you will work to garner his laugh. His sense of humor may be shaped by my many attempts to entertain him as a toddler. I'd dance, prance, make silly sounds, and hit myself upside the head with one of his toys. The slap-stick often landed him on his back, bellowing. Maybe I should have just told him knock-knock jokes.

He looks so much like his dad, a simple trip to the local laundry mat when we first arrived in Carolina would corroborate how much. I parked directly in front to unload, telling our small son to watch me out the window. Hands full, I kept my eyes on him and waved often so he'd know it. All done, I parked and unpacked my favorite little helper. He'd offer to carry something, so I watched him struggle with the liquid detergent. But he "had this" so I'd let him waddle alongside me. I never liked those scenes with the adult walking two blocks ahead of the child, as if their little legs could catch up.

Just as we were entering, a lady was leaving, so we yielded the door to each other. Out of nowhere, her eyes widened, her finger pointed, and her voice carried, "I know who his daddy is!" She had spotted our son. Continuing, she said, "Dat boy look just like his daddy!" She and I couldn't stop laughing, though my son just stared at the women making a scene. She spoke of recently meeting my husband at his job, and how blessed I was to have him. I knew that about both my husband and son!

He is tall and slender, with muscles that have started showing up from, seemingly, nowhere. He likes many sports, but has a bend towards basketball, though his legs can lunge the lengths of a track with little effort. A coach once commented that he was one of the most natural athletes he had seen in a long time, gifted with innate agility and abilities that you cannot train for or pay for. He added that our son didn't know that about himself, so pride was not his problem. He has studied my husband enough to know that arrogance is not acceptable, nor attractive.

He is the little engine that could ("I think I can. I think I can!"), always doing it in his head before actual manifestation. For a while we tried to teach him to swim, including lessons, but he rejected all such help, insisting he already knew how. To prove it, he would jump into water at pool parties and have to be helped. For some reason, he believed he could; it was just a matter of time. One day, he dove into our community pool to play with his best bud and mimicked what *he* did. To an almost frantic mom moving his way, he reared his head and gave a thumbs up that said "told ya!" He would do that for other things as well: believe, continue to declare it, then just do it.

He is growing at a pace I work to catch up with, recently resting his chin on my head and asking, "Where's Mom? Anybody see my mom?" I chuckled, but just a few days ago, it seems, that young man was a one-year-old gripping two balls inside the play land in the city that would call our name.

Back then, he liked to run back and forth under our glass dining room table. One day, I heard a thump and turned to catch him rubbing his forehead. He could no longer play his "under the bridge" game because he was too tall. That day, I couldn't help but tear up after forcing him down to nap, partly because I saw *these* days slipping away.

Universities have begun their interests in him. He has facial hair, female "friends," and fools me with the new voice that sounds like my husband's. Still the coolest adults he knows, he doesn't mind us riding together. So we've gotten to know a lot about each other over the many miles between home and school. The round trips have imparted invaluable insight into his world and the way he views things.

One day when he was a small boy, I arrived at his school and obtained quite the point of view. After rattling the normal responses to, "How was your day?" he added, "But I was a little sad." Short glances through the rear mirror were replaced by a roadside stop to see his face. Upon further examination, he put forth the details of how he had heard me say something about fasting the Sunday prior. He took it upon himself to "try" his first fast, so during lunch he'd purposed not to eat dessert. I was intrigued, staring at him as if I didn't know him. He continued to share how he triumphed in his endeavor.

All of that notwithstanding, as a mom I just wanted to know who or what had made him sad. He got to that. Before his consecration, he made one tiny mistake: he bought the biggest muffin, loaded with huge blueberries. He then set it before him and tortured himself after lunch by just looking at it, while the children at his table "downed" their desserts. At some point, he put his head on the table to lessen the "blow." When he retrieved the *source of his sadness* from his book bag, my heart was full, but I tried not to show it. I commented on what a big boy thing he had done. I added what I hoped would be life lessons: 1) Never buy a temptation and 2) Never, ever, put one where you can see it. The glad replaced the sad when he devoured that muffin *before* dinner! What? (I'm a mom!) One of the greatest testaments to my pastorate is that our little boy heard something I said and acted on it.

Today, his gifted ear is sensitive to even the slightest details in songs. He is visual, creating videos that truly capture the moment. He can dance, rap, draw, and act, but he doesn't have to be seen. I look to him while preaching when I seek a show of support. He can "play the background," and prefers to, but people follow his lead without effort. I, too, am learning to follow his examples because they are the "as a little child" ones Jesus referred to. Not the children we should *act* like, that's not what He said. The ones we should *become*. Acting bigger than our Dad could keep us outside His house.

Of sterling character, he is not expected to give a stellar performance, so he has made me angry, made me nervous, and almost made me miss my blessing. Our son, however, apologizes after a short period of time, and refuses to hold a grudge. Even while I'm sulking, he is over it and wants to talk. He is slow to anger and forgives easily. When the Lord first told me to tell him I was sorry for a rebuke, I almost passed out and passed it off as the devil! No parent of my generation apologized to their children unless a recent correction merited a visit from social services. When God insisted, I brought up my son's disobedience. He reminded me of mine, then explained that how I said what I said was the issue, not the information.

Over the years, God has included things like, "Your son is right. You are in the wrong!" Now, you know! Where was *He* when my mama spanked *me* for taking the fish out of the tank when I was innocent? He wasn't done pointing out my parenting flaws, teaching me that yelling was a lack of control, the child couldn't suffer consequences for anything that hadn't been established, and that trying to win the battle was not worth losing my son. The greatest parental advice God conferred was by faith, through grace, because of love. Believe that they will get it, try not to condemn when they don't, and so love them that they cannot find greater outside your family. I recently ordered a parent-child workshop done by educated specialists. They only affirmed what God had already taught me. They just took seven easy lessons and one sizable fee to do it!

Our son was the *only* one of our family and friends who didn't get a say in the call to assist in Carolina: he couldn't vote, offer advice, or question the decision. He was the silent partner who had to go with the majority rule. Now that he can speak for himself, I share select ministry experiences, ask his opinion, and hear his heart. Keeping this family first and our home as our sanctuary, he knows where there is solace and cherishes his personal place. Early in ministry, I established one sure edict: "I will not lose my family to church. Please don't ask me to choose." They have honored our agreement so no one crosses the threshold without invitation. And no visit is ever a pastoral problem. Our home is *not* our church! Our son is not the pastor.

> *Long before they had arcades, play stations, cell phones, video games, I-pods, Myspace, Facebook, and a Twitter account, children played. Before cabbage patches produced kids; turtles grew into teenagers; Barbie had Ken, a car, a condo, and a career, children played games. Because there were no hand-held devices or ovens that baked real cakes, they were forced to be imaginative and innovative. They created a telephone out of two Dixie cups and a string, and ate a few mud pies because "God made dirt, so dirt don't hurt."*
>
> *Back then, you played outside until the street lights came on or mama called your <u>whole</u> name. You caught lightning bugs in a Mason jar and waited until dusk to watch them light the night. You had contests to see who could take the most blackberries from the forbidden bush, then ate them until your bellies ached. You ran through streams from the water hose to cool off, or stomped in puddles from the fire hydrant when visiting your folks up north. You "Skipped to My Lou" or skipped rocks off the pond. You lay on the ground staring at clouds that seemed to show off just because you paid attention. You played hide and seek until you fell asleep and the brother who discovered you said "Mama gon' get you!"*

Some childhood games from then can help us grow up now.

- *Mother May I*—From a distance, everyone lined up facing the Mother. After she called you, a set of simple instructions followed. Before acting on them, you must get permission by asking. To move without them meant you were out.

The Object for our church: to keep our eyes on Father God and ask about everything before doing anything! To not "acknowledge Him in all our ways" is to suggest that we are grown and no longer in need of His assistance.

- *One, Two, Three, Red Light*—the set-up was similar to Mother May I. But this leader would cover his eyes, then spin around. An arm was to be extended while doing so, and the words one, two, three red light yelled out. The group would race towards the spinning leader in an effort to touch him before the last word was yelled. When the spinning stopped, whoever was caught in motion was out. The cycle would be repeated until someone touched the leader.

  The Object for our church: to touch the Lord every time we meet. In the story of the woman with the issue of blood, Jesus didn't *see* her. He *felt* her.

- *Peek-a-Boo*—the classic game you played with babies. Someone showed his face, then covered it. As the child looked for what was there, to no avail, the person removed his hands to reveal his face.

  The Object for our church: to keep asking, knocking, and seeking until we see God's face in it. Even when it seems He has gone away, we must trust that somewhere beyond the obstruction, His presence remains. Seeking God causes Him to make a special appearance. We will see Him again, because He was there all along.

- *Puncha Nella*—all participants get in a circle. The leader stands in the middle. A song dictates it's time to dance, and everyone does. At the words "So, what can you do?" the leader is free to create any movement that pleases him. The lyrics change to "And we can do it, too...," followed by an attempt from the participants to mimic the leader's example.

The Object for our church: to make Christ not just a piece of our lives, but the center: the most important part. Like the core of an apple, more is in the middle and must revolve around Him. We would have to follow His lead, because life keeps moving.

- *Hide and Seek*—Everyone hides except the leader, who counts to ten without looking. While counting, the participants scatter in an effort to find a hiding place good enough to not be discovered. The leader then begins the search, not to find everyone, just any one. If all others get to base, they are safe, but the one caught is next to lead.

  The Object for our church: to go after God. Often in Scripture He speaks of us seeking Him. Since He is never lost, what's the point? We tend to seek anything that is important to us, like the missing keys. Perhaps He wants to know where *He* is on our list of prized possessions. Also, God appreciates the chase. Whoever thought of this game must have had in mind: "I want *you* to want *me* enough to come after me." If we play, God will *let* us find Him.

Once, while taking our son to play, I reversed the question he'd asked me. "Do you like being a PK (preacher's kid)?" I asked light-heartedly, though I have learned to brace for his "don't-ask-if-you-don't-want-to-know" responses. He thought quickly, as if he'd already considered it; "Yeah, mom; It's cool. I ain't got no problems with it." The sides of his mouth cured upward. I smiled back. Then, like a child, he went to play. And I went to help the King's "kids."

CHAPTER 17

The Doctor Will See You Now

NOW ON THE *floor, you cannot ignore pungent scents of untouched meals mingled with the medicinal. You wonder if death has its own odor. The Formica looks fairly new, and certainly, clean, but the stench of disinfectant is no match for infection. Walking long halls, you search for the number you retrieved from the front desk. Pastel hues along the corridor do nothing to sooth your mood. Dosages are still waiting to be dispersed. Chemicals crowd your space.*

Almost instinctively you look into other rooms as you pass by. Some lay alone, staring out windows at things they cannot see. Others watch the moving picture, without sound. Most are in and out of sleep, sedated. They pay little attention to the foliage and may not feel much like talking to their family. This is no place for the faint of heart or weak in constitution, unless you are no visitor. In which case, this is the perfect place for you.

Sounds abound: the clang of metal, clamor of proposed "care," cries and sighs. Bells, beeps, monitors, and moaning do little to mend the sick and tired. It is hard to sleep. A recent shift change is adding to your anguish. The other person never provided what you needed; now, you have to restate your concerns and hope this one gets it right. Groaning from the gurney beside you signifies that her pain is getting worse. Today, yours is tolerable, but pain is not what brought you here. Days before, you were feeling fine. A routine visit demanded immediate attention. When your primary care professional insisted you needed intervention, she advised you to seek urgent care. You have been admitted. The hospital should help with your healing. But the only way the place can be effective is if a physician participates in the process. All cures, care, and concerns must go through him or her.

When I first heard the church being compared to a hospital, I cringed. Having a best friend diagnosed with brain cancer who later died, my high school years were spent in medical facilities. Church represented something entirely different for me. That was the place I grew, sang, danced, laughed, and met with friends. It was also where "I lived." Hospitals were not so life-giving, in my opinion. But as I matured, and my own problems surfaced, I appreciated the therapy that service provided. The parallels between church and hospital became less ambiguous.

As soon as I accepted the assignment to pastor, it was clear that pain, injury, disease, and trauma were prevalent within the congregation. Not only were maladies masked, medical attention was discouraged. It was taboo to seek professional help. Right away, I saw the need for spiritual, psychological, and emotional healing. What the old congregants had survived was enough to make anyone "sick." As the attendant on call, I would work around the clock, attempt to identify the illness, suggest a cure, prescribe the proper treatment, and follow-up.

As a new physician, I ran from one emergency to the other. Sometimes my new residency required more aide than I could provide, so I'd consult with the Chief of Staff daily. When situations got so bad that spiritual surgery was unavoidable, He'd direct me to the head surgeon. We affectionately call her Dr. A, and Descending Dove Christian Center would not be whole without her.

There are people you meet whose names you cannot recall and whose faces you cannot place, though you try intensely. But any encounter with Dr. Barbara M. Amos will make a permanent imprint. It is striking to me that two different people can be born for very divergent purposes, but each of their lives bring some crucial part the other must have. As in the movie classic "It's a Wonderful Life," you cannot imagine the vast void that would exist if they had never been born. The concept of her *not* "being" leaves gaps and holes in our story. So something had to be written about my pastor and mentor. Like her earned degrees, she has merited her own space within these pages.

My introduction to her came during my junior year in college. On campus, her name was synonymous with greatness. When my roommate began attending weekly meetings at her church, she would return to regale us with messages she'd heard by this "lady preacher." A new minister, Sister Amos was creating quite the stir. Not only was she young, and a woman, but her presentation of the gospel was so compelling that countless students were getting to wherever she was, however they could. All would tease with similar stories—they'd never heard anyone preach in such a real and relevant way. They could comprehend everything she said, wanted what she had, and looked forward to the next service. Committed to the church I served, I wouldn't abandon our assembly, but I sure was intrigued by the idea of a girl with the guts to say she was preaching the gospel.

A chance encounter would bring me to where she was. The last minute decision for a group of youth to eat at Morrison's Cafeteria in Norfolk, Virginia, was by divine design. Our church was in another city, but since this restaurant was close to home, I agreed with the usually indecisive young people. As soon as we entered, we noticed the backed-up line. Greedy and grumpy, some of our group chose to find another, less popular, place. A few of us stayed. I'm glad we did. Within the door, seated on a bench, was the new Pastor Amos. Surrounded by a couple of other women, I would have politely passed them by, until someone with us mentioned her name. Did I say mentioned? What I meant to say was acted as if they'd seen the queen! That person's excitement ignited me. Since I may never have gotten the chance again, I convinced myself to speak.

She was smaller than I'd imagined, since such big things were being said about her. Her light brown complexion was comprised of flawless skin. Her smile was quick and pleasant. Not flashy or showy, I could see from a distance that her true holiness upbringing kept her from fussing over fashion. Like any girl, she must like to look cute, but greasy make-up, gaudy jewelry, and glam were not her obsessions. She was plain, practical, and something about her was pure. Our meeting was short and sweet, and she didn't make me feel like she was just being patronizingly pastoral. I felt as if she genuinely liked people, and that made me like her right away. When I left the restaurant that Sunday, I could not foresee how our paths would ever cross again, so I savored the favor of our meeting and made my way home.

The man I was dating had joined me for church service many times. Since I was visiting his city that weekend, he requested my company where he worshipped. Arriving there presented quite the impasse. People walked briskly towards the building as if something good was inside. They came from many directions. We managed to find a parking space several blocks away. While in transit, some nodded or gave short salutations, but no one wasted time. Any member was aware that premium seats were a hot commodity. While passing, I took note of the synchronized parking attendants, warm greeters, and poised ushers. Security was making their rounds, and sound was being checked and rechecked. Every component seemed to be functioning at optimum capacity. I was pleasantly surprised, already. The man beside me was similar to the place in many ways, so I could understand his attraction to this aggregation.

With seats now filled to the overflow, singers and musicians in place, we stood to welcome clergy. I couldn't see the pastor from where we were, since standing thwarted a clear view. The men sitting in front of the pulpit assisted all females up the steps. When one extended a hand to the pastor, I saw the woman I had met in Morrison's years before. I was secretly beside myself for the privilege to finally hear her speak. Since I had stopped dodging my own destiny just a couple of years earlier, my level of anticipation was hard to veil.

I could have been anxious were it not for the powerful praise and worship that kept me fully engaged. Could it get any better? Not better, but richer and fuller! Pastor Amos, an able and anointed vessel, managed to pack so much into one message I felt I could pop! She was profound, prolific, and prophetic. Her depth of biblical knowledge and practical application were awe-inspiring. On that day, I had entered so broken, I wept the entire message. By the word's end, healing had begun. I did not attempt to speak with her that day because, frankly, I was in no condition to speak. But I did hear. I was grateful my new beau was in this type of spiritual setting. I knew he'd be fit for the Master's use. Anything his family may have instilled, this pastor would refine.

The first time I met her, we were sitting across the room from each other, preparing for marital counseling. Unlike what was customary for her, Pastor Amos agreed to perform our wedding and required time to get to know us. My new fiancé and I were humbled to have her years of prudence and guidance regarding marriage. We took our sessions seriously, doing all homework she assigned. Before we left the first meeting, she turned slightly to face the man she had impressed when calling his name as he joined the church. With so many people and so little time there, he couldn't see how she had committed his name to memory (she did that with most people). To end our shared time, she leaned in, looked sternly at him, and said, "God has blessed you, son. If you ever hurt her, I will hunt you down and !" You don't need to know what she said, but he has never forgotten it! We all laughed, but he had been "helped." So had I.

Sometime later, she stood with the minister of my childhood to give validation to our vow. The covenant service was glorious! The church was brought to its feet by the Spirit of worship, and she joined in the praise celebration. My memory of her picking up one foot and putting down the other, while trying not to dance, still makes me smile. This was supposed to be a dignified ceremony. That was the only time I recall her suppressing a shout. Honoring the man I married, we made our home at his church, Faith Deliverance Christian Center. The little lady I exchanged greetings with in a restaurant reception area was now our pastor.

At that time we were just getting acquainted; today, I could write a book! Children flock to her, men reverence her, and mothers see her as their daughter, though they will never belittle her authority. She is not where you look for sympathy when a situation demands your attention. No ticket will be purchased to attend your pity party. "The doctor" will see you on the other side of emotionalism.

A graduate of numerous colleges and universities with multiple licenses and degrees, she is one of the most intelligent people I have ever met. As a small child she consumed books, studied the encyclopedia, and read the local newspaper recreationally. Because she grew up with a father who detested ignorance and siblings who were older, time with them meant acquiring knowledge. Today, she reads newspapers daily. The best thing you can give her is a good book.

It is, also, one of her favorite things to bestow. Scholarly, she established the Faith Academy School of Excellence, which has gained prominence in fields of mathematics, science, and technology.

Business savvy, she made her own money as a teenager. She purchased her own first car and her own first home. She has made shrewd real estate investments and is astute in areas of finance and management. The recent market crisis had no ill effect on her because she had heeded a prompting of the Holy Spirit to make some adjustments.

A brilliant administrator, demanding excellence from everyone around her, she despises mediocrity. By her own admission, she concludes that anyone who works for her can work for anyone else. I agree: unable to count the many times I have had to rewrite or resubmit something for her approval. Every minutia is critiqued, as she reminds you that the term means "to make better." It is the most frustrating experience, but stretches you past your normal potentialities.

Gifted and talented, she plays many instruments well. The ability to grasp complex musical material granted her the privilege, when she was just a young woman, to serve as percussionist for the renowned Shirley Caesar. A music major, the youthful Amos's skills weren't exactly what the singer required. She didn't need a "horn-player, but a drum beater." Not easily discouraged, Sister Amos purchased a set of drums and taught herself to play. She was hired and began traveling extensively. With a sensitive ear, she can hear even the slightest straying from what was intended. An acute eye for architecture, she meticulously designed the church and school she founded.

Although she has little leniency for "stupid," her sense of humor is hysterical. Her comedic story-telling and clever anecdotes are the stuff of legends. I wish I had recorded them all. Anyone around her in casual company expects to laugh, and loudly. She delivers the unsuspecting punch line with a serious face, rarely laughing, while you try to pick yours off the floor. When something is funny to her, the room can hardly be contained.

Prophetic, though careful not to advertise and put up a tent, everything she has ever spoken to us has come to pass. Some things, at the time she spoke them, skirted absurdity. She is discerning without acting deep. Upon her first visit to our church, a sudden prompting caused her to leave the service. Unsure of her well-being, I sent after her. She was discovered on the side of the building. She wasn't alone. A man was walking around vehicles sprinkling something. In the African-American culture, such acts are often forms of root-working or witchcraft. He stopped when he realized he had been exposed. It didn't take! The first thing she forth told us is unfolding while I'm writing this book. The words she called us up to speak in our ears, one Friday night years ago, could only have come from another place. She was convinced enough to repeat what God said.

Whatever is said of her, there must also be this—she is always the same. She doesn't have wild mood swings. She is consistent, steady, with strong conviction. What she said yesterday has not changed. You cannot make her back down, back track, or back into a corner. There is no need trying. That doesn't make her unreasonable, it makes her stable. With narcissistic leadership, you never know what's coming next. With her, you always do. Her integrity will govern the outcome. To her, right is just right!"

She doesn't mind a good fight, if it involves "the least of these," so she champions causes that include the disadvantaged. To that, she is a missionary first, with a passion for Haiti in particular. So anointed is she to fulfill this assignment that not even strange foods, bed bugs, or sweltering heat can dissuade her. Generous gifts are lavished on those who cannot help themselves. Impassioned for outreach, her finances are used to fund such endeavors. Substance abuse, homelessness, poverty, and injustice will always have her support and her heart.

Faithfully serving under the late presiding Amy B. Stevens of the Mount Sinai Holy Churches of America, Pastor Amos was consecrated as Bishop, going on to earn a doctorate in ministry. She was later appointed prelate, overseeing southern states. When God showed me the exit door from the organization, I wasn't sure how it might reshape our relationship. But a strange series of events would find her outside the group, despite the deepest desire of its leader.

I was saddened for her, but grateful that we would still maintain connectivity.

With absolutely no aspiration to be famous, she humbly released the great church she founded into the capable command of its minister of music, Sharon S. Riley. The move was unprecedented and unexpected. Everyone was thrown, including Minister Riley, and few knew what the outcome of such a move would produce. We all hoped it was God! So sure was He that the church has not only survived, but thrived, exceeding all expectations. So sure was she that she stepped down and stepped up to the plate to assist a strained minister in the small North Carolina town of Kinston.

The time I first met Pastor Amos, she was traveling in ministry, both within the United States and abroad. Most people in the gospel music world knew her name. She had spoken at all the major venues and conferences, so her gifts were in great demand. The first female African-American pastor to grace the cover of *Charisma* magazine, she was highly sought to bring credibility and stability to the concept of women's roles in ministry. Her office still receives hundreds of calls requesting she make an appearance.

The threat of stardom, because she knows how flesh handles fame, fueled her decision to retreat from the road. She selected, rather, to give herself wholly to the less-glamorous grind of ministering to hurting people right where they are. She committed to covering a small band of merry men and women we call Faith Deliverance Christian Fellowship. Each of us is gifted, distinct, and versatile. Competition among us is discouraged, so we have learned to celebrate the others' success. We love God and this union. We are autonomous, but accountable. Together, we are determined to exalt the King and His kingdom.

As much as she has to her credit, Dr. Amos doesn't have to be seen, but you will not soon forget what she says. The gift of exaltation enables her to speak a befitting word in and out of season. The gift of "helps" empowers her to speak directly, honestly and sometimes sharply. The two-edged sword she wields is the same one she has used in many spiritual surgeries. "The Doctor" is anointed to make precision cuts, and trained not to leave you open. She will suture you when through. Though a scare may remain, the pain will not.

I have been under her knife more times than I care to share. Personal and professional slashes or strain could not go unattended. When I failed to use preventative measures, damage or disorder caused me to call "the doctor." I was sent to North Carolina as a general practitioner, new to the people, place, and all things pastoral. But every person can use a physician. Even doctors need doctors. So in my general practice, sometimes I needed attention. Sometimes I needed a specialist, and for that, I would have to call Dr. Barbara Marie Amos.

CHAPTER 18
First Gentleman?

I HAVE DEFINITELY SAVED the best person for last—like the delectable dessert—the main attraction—the special guest of honor.

The man whose blood runs through me (Doug); the man who made my altar call (John); the man who encouraged my song (Arlie); the man who drove my family to *every* church service for years (Jimmie); the man who made me believe I was a teacher (Leon); the man who convinced me to apply for college (Ken); the man who granted me sanctuary while I was there (Ernie); and the man who listened to my stories (Odell); are men I highly esteem. Tucker, Harper, and Johnson are the big brothers I exalt. They never used me, abused me, or underestimated me. They are all pastors today, and that, of course, is funny to me. The last laugh is theirs I'm sure.

Other men have impacted my life, but none *so* much as the one I am pleased to share my life with. He is my husband, Antonio E. Wellington, and he is all of what I wanted and more than I dreamed I'd ever have. Since I know him like a book, I am qualified to quantify.

He is the nicest man you could ever meet, genuinely glad to make your acquaintance. I've lost count of the times we've been interrupted over dinner for someone to tell something kind about him I already know. Their initial impression was correct, and I concur. Because he is so likable, I'd question the mental state of anyone who said they didn't.

He is good-looking, well-groomed, and there's nothing generic about him. He is maple syrup-brown and sweet as southern tea, but reserves all his "suga'" for home. There, he is the dream weaver, determined to make our dreams his delight. I am slow to speak of any desire because I know he will work to make it my reality.

His word is bond, so he does not practice speaking out of both sides of his mouth. The life and death on his tongue are serious weapons he doesn't fire for sport. He is a stickler for veracity, desiring the story to be told *right*. Though joyful, to the point of jubilance, he is careful of jargon or idle jesting. By his words, our family has seen the incredible, and our church has done the impossible.

He is extremely intelligent, greatly gifted, and properly trained. Educated and an exceptional actor, he was accepted into programs to work with politicians, and has awed us with unparalleled performances. I enjoy acting with him more than anyone, but he is no fraud. He could boast of much, but I have *never* heard him exalt himself.

He is an extraordinary husband, father, friend, and fellow-laborer. Men want to be like him, children look up to him, and women know they are safe in his company. He is the son every mother wants, the neighbor you hate to see move, the employee who will run your business like it's his. He will work longer than is required, but play harder when it's done.

He is cordial, considerate, and compassionate. He is a cut up, a clown, and the life of any party. But he will relinquish the floor so he can appreciate another's gift. His jokes are belly-achingly funny, and his stories are animated. Loving life, he is easy going, laid back, and non-combative, but do not take that as weakness. His strength is in his ability to command his spirit and stay connected to the Spirit. He prays "just because," witnesses anywhere, keeps the Word around him, and any real worship can find him on his face. It is easy to follow him because he has already been where we want to go. There is no need to lead by brute strength because his influence is inferred.

You wouldn't know he is a preacher because he doesn't wear a backwards collar, never talks "churchy," refuses to keep saying "doc" to people who are not, and includes the "invisible" women in a mostly male room. The men of our city look forward to his barbershop appointments because he addresses his comments to the room and gives them Jesus in bite sizes they can digest. His comedic timing has made him a staple. His un-churched barber does him the honor free of charge, just to keep him coming back.

We clap when he enters our home, not because he demands it, but because our child thinks he deserves it. It is a small token of our admiration and affection. He never has to select his own clothes. It is my pleasure to keep him pressed. He gets the chicken breast, only slice of leftover cake, and last drop of juice, though he will fight to give it away. His promise to live trying to out-serve me has not been broken.

Disciplined, he does the same thing over and over, just because it is the right thing to do. A discriminating eater who refuses to gluttonize, he will leave one half of a cookie or one third of milk. But he has a ferocious appetite for anything God or the power of His Spirit. An avid reader, he consumes three or four books at a time. When he was first introduced to Christianity, he heard several ministers make the statement, "You know the story," during their delivery. He said he didn't have a clue what they were referring to, so he found a book on children's Bible stories and started to familiarize himself with them.

Anyone who knows him will echo my sentiment. He is due this honor, because he gave me space to stretch my wings and sore. Since he is not insecure, I could fly without fear of falling. He would make sure I never hit the bottom. I owe him so much, but he has required very little. He has covered me, clothed me, counseled me, and cuddled me through the best and worst of times. He is not perfect, but he is *the perfect man* for me. I love him dearly and sincerely, and he knows it. And I'm just getting started.

When we started out, he was not a pastor, nor did he want to be. Just as well, because I had *absolutely* no desire to be married to one, let alone *be one*. I also didn't desire to be a first lady, since they were some of the most unhappy people I personally knew. Their husbands had determined their place long ago and demanded they stay put. Many were bitter, resentful, never satisfied, but just too "sanctified" to leave. So they spent their lives role playing. She was to be the best dressed, sit where she could be seen, stand when he spoke, and never share his secret.

Some have been over-used or under-used, abused, and bruised long ago. They are still together, but his ministry is *his life*, and she knows it. A dear bishop once, shamefully, shared with us that the church had become his "mistress." Many pastors' wives walk steps behind their husbands, don't speak unless they're spoken to, and smile in spite of it. I hurt for these first *line of defense* ladies, knowing that if there is more in her, she could be an asset, not just an accessory—a true help meet (fit) for him. They could hold up a light and do serious damage to the domain of darkness together. Although gifted to act, I do not pretend well, so I surely would have stopped that sideshow *before* it went on the road.

At the time I met my husband, I was already traveling as an evangelist in ministry. He volunteered to serve as my manager, making sure the good ole' boys didn't take advantage of me. They still tried. That was as close as I ever wanted to be to the "telephone." For more, God would have to "call" someone else.

We met after I emceed a live gospel recording at Miracle Temple in Newport News, Virginia. Neither one of us wanted to be there. I made all attempts to cancel because I wasn't feeling well, and he tried not to attend upon being invited. Both efforts failed because being here *now*, required being there *then*. After hours of taping and re-taping, the project was complete and I collected my things to leave. We began in the evening, and now it was the early hours of morning, so I could hardly wait to say my fond farewells.

A sharply-dressed gentleman made his way to where I was greeting guests. Patiently biding his time, he was next in line. "Wellington, Antonio Wellington." was his opening statement, spoken well. I thought, "Bond, James Bond," then followed his very clean fingernails to his very handsome face. A stunning smile exposed gleaming teeth, the kind of commercials. I smiled back and listened to his request. He had some dealings in the music industry, his reason for coming, and wanted my contact information to discuss the matter further. *Yeah, right! Music* industry, my foot! Something *in* him liked something *about* me. At the time I didn't know how much.

We had attended the same university and lived across the street from each other. Our paths rarely crossed, but *when* they did, I don't recall. He never forgot. On one such occasion, I emceed a gospel concert that he attended. He said he spoke to me afterwards, but there is no recollection on my part. Another time, he saw me outside an apartment complex and made a u-turn to find out which building I lived in. Neither: I was just visiting. He knew *my* name, but would have to wait years for me to know *his*.

Now, Antonio was before me, and I had given him my information.

To celebrate the exchange he offered to escort me to my vehicle. I draped a black cashmere coat with fox collar over my arms and headed towards the exit. In the foyer I felt enough "hawk" (blistering cold) to stop acting cute, so I began to wrap myself in the coat I carried. He assisted, like someone with good home training. *And I let him,* like someone with good house-keeping training.

Outside, he sure didn't act like it was sub-zero, though clad in the heaviest and longest leather I'd ever seen. Since my good friend had talked me into coming by agreeing to drive, he opened her door, too. As I settled back into my seat, I had the strangest thought: *That's going to be your husband.*

Whose talking to me and why? was my subsequent thought. I had just started paying close attention to the voice of God and believed this to be His. If this *was* some kind of prophetic insight, I wanted a witness.

Wellington, Antonio made his closing statement and closed my door. When he did, I told my friend not to pull off until I could speak. My heart was racing, as was my head. "I need to tell you something, chil', so if it comes to pass, you know God told me. I believe He said that *that* man is going to be *my* husband!" She screamed in my ear, and then calmed down long enough to insert, "Did the Lord say he has a brother?" We "hollered," laughing the long road home. The rest, as they say, is his-story. He is detailed and determined not to leave anything out. What I *will* say is we married, *just like God said,* and are bound by a love covenant that is sustaining. The greatest gift to our marriage has been the Holy Spirit flowing between us.

Reared in Pentecost, I was introduced to Holy Spirit baptism early. I would encounter Him when I was twelve and have lived with Him ever since. At the time Antonio and I met, he knew of no such experience and believed he had everything God was giving. One night, following one of our first dates, he pulled into the driveway to escort me to the door. Before we got out, I asked the question that had been on my heart for a while. "Have you been baptized in the Holy Ghost?" He confidently responded, "Yes." Still unsure, I didn't rebuke or refute him; I merely asked if he had a minute for me to share something with him. "Of course," he said, adjusting his seat to pay full attention.

I spoke of my new birth, then added what happened when I received "my birthday gift," the baptism in the Holy Ghost. At my conclusion, he softly spoke, "No. Nothing like that has ever happened to me. But if God is giving something away, I want it. Just show it to me in His Word." I respected that. Before I did, I asked what *kind* of church he attended. He had only been there a short period of time and wasn't quite sure of my inference. When he mentioned that he had heard his pastor speak in tongues, I suggested he go to Bible Study and inquire.

Following his first class, a brother compelled Antonio to stay for a second session when the larger church group splintered into smaller ones. This night would feature the first male study. Before the class could get off to a good start, someone asked the teacher about the Holy Spirit baptism. Antonio sat straight up, sensing this was no mere coincidence. Before the night was over, he was ready, willing, and available. They dismissed class, planning to pick up the discussion next time. The most interested student didn't want to wait that long.

Memorial Day would find him back at my mother's, trying to "knock the door down." When it was opened, he began speaking right away. He was "ready to receive!" So where could he go, and what did he need to do, and who could help him? My mother was stirred by his sincerity and got on the telephone right away. While she did, I checked his heart and motives. I wanted to make sure he didn't feel coaxed or rushed. I also wanted to be sure he wasn't trying to win me over. He'd already done that.

A dear friend of my mother, who was no novice to altar work, showed up within moments. She checked his readiness then transported him to the home of another friend, since we lived far from church, and it was a holiday. When they left, I escaped to shower. While in the bathroom, I thought this as good a time as any to make my request known. I began to pour out what had been locked in. I told my Father how much I loved Antonio, and how nice it would be if he knew, experientially, what life *through* the Spirit was like.

No sooner had I uttered, "Please fill him," when a shout from downstairs penetrated the running water. It was my mother strongly urging me to "Pick up the upstairs phone!" When I did, I heard my future husband, not just speaking in tongues, but filled to overflow! He had received within moments, effortlessly, easily. What had taken me years of tarrying, and some turmoil, was his just for the asking. Within the first year of being filled, he helped over one hundred others get their gift without labor. He made that his minimal objective. We have, since, *lost count*. He walks people through that experience easily and effectively, the way he received.

On this highway of shared ministry we have learned to stay in our own lanes. When it's time to change lanes, we rehearse applying blinkers as a courtesy. Most importantly, I have been in the driver's seat long enough to know when to use the same lane, following *his* lights. On occasion, we have been detoured, pulled over to the pit for help, and stopped for driving too fast. But for the most part, we yield the right of way and respect the other's hours behind the wheel, supervised class, and license to drive. The road hasn't always been smooth, and we've hit our share of potholes.

Shortly before leaving the old royal blue country church, I began to have a repeating thought, nudge, prod. Each time, it became louder and stronger. I had been down that road enough times to take note, so, like Mary, I stored it away. At the time, I didn't know that our exodus was imminent, so I continued preaching, planning, and preparing for the next chapter. One day that *thing* interrupted every other thing, demanding my observation and obedience.

My husband had done anything he could to maximize our ministry: ushered, cleaned, led praise and worship, taught Sunday School, learned to play "shout music," been our driver, prayed us through, and let me "shine." He was content, and intent on, serving *the anointing*, not just *the appointment*. An armor-bearer book had taught him to do that well, but training had taken place in a four year course at our church.

At home, I was his "girl," his "baby," his "boo." I did not boss him, manipulate him, or attempt to minimize him. He had the final say, but appreciated my assessment. At church I was *his* pastor. At first, the roles seemed reversed, and we fought rumors that I "wore the pants." We didn't know of *one* other couple with our dynamic, though some co-labored. There was no *first gentleman* to whom we could refer, so everything had to be learned firsthand. God had to make the way plain and straight, securing us in the process. It was progressive and hard.

One day the *thing* abruptly interrupted me, so I had to speak. I had been spoken to, and the seriousness in God's voice proved time sensitive, though I didn't know why. I had filed it away for so long because it was the last thing either one of us wanted to hear. The thought frightened me, concerned me, and disturbed me because I did not want it to mess us up. I wondered if that's how *male* pastors felt. I called to confer with my pastor.

At the conclusion of our conversation, I was clear. The next Sunday morning, I made the announcement: the appointment. My husband would also be pastor. The church erupted in praise and applause. They rose to their feet in thunderous ovation and remained that way for a while. They seemed to have known my secret. I had not even shared it with him. He sat still, stunned, though not surprised.

Long walks and talks later, he would reveal that he had struggled with that intimation for months, but wanted it to go away. He was first made aware of such a call five years earlier! At one point, the situation got so serious that he told God he would only pastor if God told me. Antonio thought that would conclude the matter. He knew how much I hated the idea, and figured I would repel it—never wanting to act on it. I had done just that, but soon repented because God proved, repeatedly, that He knew the way He was taking us. Within months of the announcement, the *new* church was birthed. I should have known. It would stand to reason. It made so much sense:

In the natural order of things, most people comprehend the necessity of two parents. As the product of a single parent family, I cannot be more grateful for my mother's nurture, but missed the contributions of a father. That lack created vicious voids and vices. Even where there are successful single parents, there is deficit. What fathers and mothers possess is sundry and complimentary. What they provide is balance. Neither can *be* the other, and children who grow up with the blessing of both tend to fare better. That is the way God designed the family to function. So even if we have done it another way, we must admit that doing it His way is best. My husband and I began to pastor like spiritual parents. In parenting, two sides of the same coin are accepted and even expected.

The "children" would have to learn to adjust as well, and that would take time and *intentional* effort. Almost immediately some tried to play us, pitting one against the other. They would corner us, getting one answer they didn't like, before seeking the other answer that sounded more suitable. They would play "he said, she said" until we got our game plan straight. We would never advice, pray, or meet with anyone alone. We would discuss *everything*.

Because we both are vocal, we had to rehearse *not* speaking over each other at home. I messed this up more times than I can calculate. But recording after recording would prove that I could out-talk him, so I was the one who had to practice being quiet. In addition, in our church, I had been the primary spokesperson for so long that simmering-down had to be a conscience endeavor. While in pause, I would also have to fight playing what I was going to say next in my head. The thoughts would thwart my attention, making what he said of less importance. The Holy Spirit would have to remind me, often.

Jealousy is cruel and consistent. It creeps up on you, unaware. Because my husband and I are diverse in some ways, people often managed to exalt one, while putting down the other. One was "alright," but the other was "great!" One "blessed," but the other "changed their lives!" One "prayed," but the other "called down heaven!" One was "gifted," but the other was "glorious!"

We had to learn to tell each other when we felt slighted, even when it sounded insecure. We had to affirm that we were not in competition, but communion. We had to render ourselves useless without God enabling us both. We had to direct each compliment upward—not with our fingers, but with our hearts. I checked, often, to see how *we* were doing.

Years prior, while hearing prophetic utterances relative to *my* call, my husband posed a private *What about me?* to God. He was unsure what part he was to play in all the Lord was planning. At the moment of his thought, the prophet stopped mid-sentence and turned to him. "And, Antonio, for taking care of your wife, the Lord is going to give you *whatever* you desire." He has!

The new pastor Antonio merely continued everything he was already doing. He was the undisputed encourager and enforcer. He had been leading, teaching, praying, witnessing, working the business of church, administering Holy Spirit baptism, and believing for miracles. One would come in a most atypical way.

We all knew he was courageous, but this would cross the line to outrageous! The members of old church had named a dog Sinai. He was a stray—scraggly and scrawny. We didn't know who he belonged to, where he came from, or where he went after service. But each time we showed up, so did he: to receive his scraps and welcome the attention. With a touch of OCD (obsessive compulsive disorder), I could have done without him scratching, but the saints seemed to like our informal mascot.

One day, while we were all on in front of the old church laughing, talking loud, and leaving, my husband *hit* Sinai! Everyone responded, even those who didn't care for the mutt. He was *our* dog, and none of us wanted him to die! There he was, wedged under the front wheel. My husband backed up, then jumped out to see Sinai—still and suffering. We stood, helpless, but the man of God needed space. A recent read by an author named David Duell gave him the boldness he needed. He laid hands on *the dog*! You read it write... *the dog*! Then, he began to pray with as much fervor as any father in a life threatening situation. Sinai jumped to his paws and ran-off. Healed! We stood in shock! The dog would be back for the next service, and the next. As far as I know, he is *yet* alive and well. Ironically, a young lady from our church nicknamed my husband PAW for Pastor Antonio Wellington. Maybe we owe the credit to that dog-gone Sinai.

He has been the pastor you want other pastors to be. Not easily ruffled, he refuses false responsibility, so the church belongs to *Jesus*. He was the One Who founded it upon solid composition and promised nothing would prevail against it. With that assurance, Pastor Antonio is free to pastor from an informal perspective. He is always jovial when he enters the room. Everyone is glad to see him as he makes his rounds, waving and speaking. Senior saints are lit up as he shakes their hands or kisses mothers' foreheads. Children wait as close to the edge of their seat as possible. Their eyes grow huge as he lays hands on them or passes out high fives. They chuckle when he moves on, looking at each other like, "Did he get you?" This happens before *every* service. He is not the pastor you duck.

"Paw" has a unique way of making people feel *they* matter. Usually, it's unconventional. Sometimes, it's unbelievable. Once, after service, I caught him pushing a man in his wheelchair down the ramp. Seems nice, right? I need to add, that it was at NASCAR speed! In the parking area, the pastor popped a wheelie to end the show. The man who thought he was getting assistance and all the spectators were losing it. I almost did as well, but I wasn't laughing. To pacify me, he bent down to look in the face of the passenger. "He loves it! Don't you?" provoking the other half of the circus act. The man couldn't answer between laughter and tears. That *must* have broken some code in the pastor's handbook (that must be why we don't have one). He only lives by one book anyway.

A glutton for a good giggle, my husband, the pastor, challenged the man who had a stroke to arm wrestle. He was "game." Together, they entertained the men of our ministry during their Super Bowl party. I can only speculate, at this point, because I wasn't present, and the details are still sketchy. What *is* clear is that the pastor lost! What is murky is that he said he "let the man win." Whenever asked why he would let the man win, he only replies, "How would it look for the pastor to take advantage of the guy who has issues?" After laughing at that same statement, the "winner," repeatedly, challenges him to a rematch.

We match each other well. When I had the nagging notion of our ministry being a two-headed monster, God gently reminded me that my husband and I are one, not two. He has designed us in perfect symmetry. When I am weak, he is strengthened. When he is unsure, I am made certain. When we are empty, the Holy Spirit fills us. Nothing about this story would work without him. He was the first gentleman. With no maps or directions, he refused to keep driving without asking. God has guided him through hills and valleys, winding roads, missing bridges, and rubber-necking. He has become an incomparable under shepherd: salient and substantial. *As one*, we are moving in destiny. He is the *gentle man* I am honored to put *first*.

CHAPTER 19

I Told the Storm

WE LIVE IN a beach community. From any direction, a short drive will land you on sandy shores. Four beaches at your front door come with perks: tourists, the television and movie industry (our city is called "Lil' Hollywood"), and top chefs catering to discriminating tastes. But there have also been less inviting "visitors." With warm weather and waves sometimes comes the threat of storms. We have survived scores of them, but most people have. I do not wish to celebrate surviving, but the success of *speaking.* These are *our* storm stories.

"FURIOUS FLOYD"

The weather reports, quite frankly, were frightening. A tropical storm had reached hurricane status and was heading straight for the east coast of North Carolina. *Wait a minute, that's where we live!* Hurricane Floyd was a madman! His projected arrival triggered the third largest evacuation in the history of the country. Telephone calls began pouring in from family and friends who wanted to know our intentions, since we hadn't live in Wilmington that long. There was so much movement. Stores were running out of basic supplies, and neighbors were boarding up and rolling out. No one was doing "nothing." We strongly considered an exodus ourselves, but another telephone call altered our plans.

One family from our congregation lived in a singlewide trailer and had no idea where they'd ride out the storm. Thinking there may be others, I suggested the use of our old cinderblock church for shelter. We would let them in, leave the key, and head for the inland. But the more I packed, the guiltier I became. I felt like the captain abandoning ship, so I stopped to pray. My husband assisted with the answer, slowly agreeing to stay at the church with anyone who wanted to. I'm sure his first concern was for the safety of our family.

Most people opted to remain home because they had endured

many storms. I would make sure the ones who spent the night at our church were well cared for. I drove around our city diligently seeking emergency items, food, drinks, snacks, baby products, and games. I was set to make the best of this dire situation. Everyone was already afraid, so I took it upon myself to make it fun. I found candles, kerosene lamps, and flashlights, since power outages were already predicted.

At church, we welcomed families, friends, and anyone seeking safety. Next, I sent word down and across the street to inform the older neighbors that they didn't have to be alone. Not long after the last person was in, the bottom fell out. Rain alone is seldom threatening, but the wind soon picked up. Over the next few hours, darkness dominated the day. The small group of us ate a lot, snacking for no reason. I discovered Welch's fruit snacks that night and almost drank them. I later concluded that much of the binge eating was storm stress. We prayed, sang, and played. But Floyd was not in the mood for games. He raged, rattled the windows, and revved up his engine. And this was just his pre-show!

We tried to remain encouraged, but the howl of the wind and the wail of the rain suggested this was going to be a *very* long night. As new to storms as I was to ministry, I was apprehensive for the members who were hunkered down in their not-so-stable dwellings, and for us. It's interesting how hearing something can be just as bad as seeing it. Cinderblock seemed no match for the maniac outside. After dinner, we talked and told each other stories, trying to deafen the sounds. The flickering lights signaled a turn, and all of our faces showed it.

To counter, we decided to pray again, but not before lighting many candles. This prayer was not like the opening one; this time we meant business, binding any devastation to anyone or anything associated with us. Then, we worshipped, petitioned, and sought Father God in ways that caused Him to come see what all the fuss was about. Prior to that night, we had been graced by His glory *often*. But that midnight madness would mark the beginning of holy ground encounters. Praise, from a place of desperation, is different—filled with self-abandonment. When we "came around," nothing outside had changed; in fact, Floyd was acting worse. But everyone inside was at peace. So sound were we that people began to claim their spots for sleep.

My husband, having worked a long twelve hours, collected our son and retired to the small pastor's study to rest. I would have joined them, but there were a few people still up, so I felt obliged. Storms tend to "show out" most during the night. I once heard a teaching on the various night watches, which explained the high activity of the demonic during certain times. That night would agree with such theories.

A small band of us braved the night to gather in the church's foyer. Standing before the glass doors, we saw what we had heard for all those hours. Floyd was in town, and he was the company you wished would leave. Before our eyes, he was wreaking havoc; trash cans, bicycles and other large items were tossed about like toys. Houses were missing parts, lawns were missing furniture. Trees were toppled like toothpicks, making snapping sounds as they surrendered.

One thing after the other swept by. Debris spun and swirled. We were in shock! I was stiff, seeing how furious Floyd was. No one who saw what we saw could honestly attribute such devastation to the Divine. This, clearly, was not His doing. At some point we retired, but we would never forget the stormy night we spent with the formidable Floyd.

We welcomed morning. In its wake, the storm had left damage, destruction and demise. But each report that came in confirmed that everyone we knew was safe and sound. It was still strongly advised that no one take to the roads, since power lines were down and flood waters were rising. We would *not* heed the warning for two main reasons: the neighborhood we lived in was prone to mass floods, and we lived across the street from a pond. The other reason had to do with the fact that the people in our church could not return to their home, if one existed. They would need more food and supplies until further notice.

My husband and I made the difficult decision to brave the rapids because we believed that's what a good pastor would do. I could, easily, have felt like the bird Noah released. I desired to be the dove. The saints waved us off without trying to look too concerned. We waved back, thinking this would be an uneventful search and siege. Boy, were we wrong!

Sunshine is a deceptive sight after a storm. It suggests that the worst has passed. The streets near the church were riddled with trash and once-treasured possessions, but passable. I spoke too fast. The road that would have taken us to the highway was "out!" The White Stocking area had water up to the windows of houses and would take *years* to recover. Not to worry, we turned around and headed for the back road, Route 117. Several towns separated our church from our home. Passing through them was pitiful. The scene resembled some sick fairy tale after a demented giant had stomped the village. We drove slowly, sorrowfully. Many of these residents were left with little to rummage through, their livelihoods ruined.

We arrived at the entrance of our neighborhood much later than usual. And as presumed, flood waters greeted us when we turned onto our street. We parked at a point and walked the rest of the way, with our baby bouncing. I had thought of leaving him with those at church, but quickly dismissed the notion when I considered what he, too, had just endured. We should be together. I could only imagine what was lurking in the waters we waded through, but I was grateful our son was high above it, resting on Daddy's shoulders. Some neighbors selected the safer water rafts to inventory.

With the exception of water up to our garage, all was well on the home front. Salvaging any food or supplies, we splashed back to our vehicle. The day before, we had to drive over a portion of our neighbor's property because the street was flooding. A lawn lover, we knew he would not take too kindly to the desperate decision. But we hoped he would understand, under the circumstances. This day, we had to walk through part of his yard to reach ours. He would be waiting when we walked back, yelling something that I'm sure included a curse word or two. The statement I heard clearly, "You should have left sooner!" proved how much he valued his hydrangeas over human life. Since he was never the most hospitable, we were pleased to be rid of the hostility, his words at our backs. He would not be our only adversary that day.

An attempt to return the way we had come failed. In the short period of time we had stopped by our home, roads were more treacherous. We detoured towards the highway. The way ahead looked better, but things are seldom what they seem. Interstate 40 had a small river running across it. Vehicles were stuck on both sides, but most were making it. Because we had the van, we decided to advance.

Following the path left by the vehicle before us, we cautiously continued. Nearing the exit to our church, the wake being created by the car in front of us made waves for our van. The sudden surge covered the hood and windshield, temporarily impairing visibility. This wave from the long gone guide car, left waves of panic in our vehicle. My husband made the drastic mistake of taking his foot off the accelerator and applying the brakes. When he did, the engine sputtered, and then stalled! We were stuck! Rushing water crashed against both sides of our van! On my side, I could see the level rising too close to the door. I looked back at our son entertaining himself, oblivious to the danger we all faced. I tried to think of how we could escape: who would carry what, where was the water shallow? The thought created more uneasiness. God would have to help us!

Beside me, my husband and father of the baby behind us, was out of sorts. We both could hear what sounded like the muffler filling up, and we both knew that wasn't good. Something must happen soon, or we could be swept away! Failed attempts to restart the engine were made worse by the water coming our way. To combat compound drowning images, we prayed—in different ways. Mine was spiritual; his was "street." To my prayer of supplication, he added, "Come on, Jesus, Baby! You can do it!" If we were not in the middle of a crisis, I would have viewed that as comedy at its best, but I knew the distressed place from which it flowed.

If ever he needed a help mate, it was now. I *pretended* calm, and placed my hand on his shoulder for comfort. "Baby, calm down. We're gonna be alright," I said as softly as I could make myself say it. He glanced at me briefly, then gave it one more go, believing what I was still struggling with. To my amazement, the van cranked up, and we were on our way! The rest of the ride was a praise service. When we testified to the church dwellers, someone commented, "That's why we had to pray for ya'll, all of a sudden!" Floyd had bullied, bluffed, and blew his way through, trying to divide and conquer our family. But we refused to let him do all the talking. We discovered that we had something to say that day...even to a storm. And we would have to do it again.

"Fun in the Son"

We were cleaning up from our Resurrection baptism and Holy Communion when word came that it was raining. That was an understatement! A torrential downpour had come out of nowhere. I left the men to lock up the fabulous Rock Church, which had been family enough to let us use their baptistery and sanctuary. Unable to hardly see due to poor visibility, I called my husband to ask his opinion about canceling the second part of our plans. Now most church folks would have cancelled their own plans, but not our troopers. Some were already in route to the cook out site for "Fun in the Son." We had anticipated this event for so long that they simply "didn't have time for that."

For some odd, only God, reason, that none of us was clear about, the brother who my husband asked to drive ahead and relay the message had a suggestion of his own. "Why don't we just go out there, anyway?" If you knew Bro. Jacobs, you would know how unlikely his comment was. He is Mr. Pragmatic; logical and rational to the point of needing his own faith stretched. We have worked to get him to see the bigger picture in more than one instance. He is still unsure of why he said what he said that day.

Requiring minor motivation, my husband came in agreement with the lone Bro. Jacobs. With that, he rallied the rest of the troops with his "On to the park." Now, you know I didn't need to be there, because I may have considered committing both of them. I had gone home to get addition items, intending to meet everyone at the park. The sky before and behind gave me cause for pause. Clouds grew thicker and blacker, intruding upon the sun that welcomed this day. Closer to home, I could not ignore the similarities to the classic *Wizard of Oz*. This was more than a passing rain.

At the park, mud was everywhere, or, at least, that's what I heard. The men brought out a smoke grill that resembled a black barrel sawed in half. The grill provided by the park was overflowing. My husband asked that ours be placed under the shelter—proving he was, in fact, from the city. I'm sure they could feel the rain drops falling about them, but none made mention. Anyone would have easily questioned their own sanity based on our busyness. Either we were naïve or fighting the good fight of faith. Maybe we had just anticipated the day, so eating in the rain would be just as good as "singing in the rain." At any rate, everyone kept moving.

My husband assigned four people to move to the four corners of the park and "Speak to the storm: north, south, east, and west." We had taught on the believers authority from the Bible, so he thought this was a good time to see if we had any. Those who weren't setting-up watched from their *dry* vehicles. The storm speakers were, themselves, young and impressionable, interested in being the instruments of a modern miracle. They spoke with boldness and confidence, binding and loosing. They told the devil where to go because they had been taught that storms can have a demonic dimension that was often falsely attributed to God (as was the case with the Biblical Job).

I'm sure to the casual observer we would have looked out-of-our-minds, but because it was storming, no one was present to object. The storm watchers were challenged to believe past the lack of visibility. While they were fighting their own eyes, my husband was fighting his own ears. He "heard" the words, "What kind of pastor are you! You have these people out here thinking they can stop the rain! Even if it did stop, the ground would be too wet to play or enjoy the day!"

My husband reconsidered, believing he had come to *his senses*. He had not paid attention to the statements "*they* can stop" or "even *if* it did." Had he, he would have realized that we knew we were not *The Stopper*. Also, the *if* may have clued him to the truth that these were not his own words. Someone knew how close we were to a breakthrough. The accuser added, "You are just being irresponsible!" Knowing how determined we were to be "good pastors," that accusation persuaded my husband to retreat.

He approached the first speaker, but could not bring himself to tell him he had done a good enough job. The young man was full throttle, commanding the elements to "obey the word of God," and telling the storm to "cease and desist." That young man was doing what he been taught, and he *expected* results. Reaching one hand toward his shoulder, Pastor Antonio jerked it back, moving away to say, "Lord, I can't." And it's a good thing he didn't. Within moments of not silencing the speaker, the rain suddenly stopped, as if a faucet had been turned off! The watchers surfaced from their vehicles adding the food, fun, and fellowship this event lacked. Even more, the sun burst through the clouds and dried up all the rain, right where they were.

There's a lot to be said about being at the right place, at the right time, with the right people, doing the right thing. I had missed all four. I was still home, waiting on the locksmith to unlock my front door. Finally inside, away from the raging wind and relentless rain, I called my husband to check his estimated time of arrival. I was concerned about their safety as I watched the weather get worse.

When I asked where he was, he informed me that he and everyone else were at the park. That couldn't be possible, I conjectured, since we lived about ten minutes away. And where I was, there was no letting up. He insisted it wasn't that way at the park and suggested I "Come and see what the Lord has done." I had to! The closer I got, the clearer the sky became. At Castle Hayne Park, we played, ate, danced, competed, and laughed till dusk. That Resurrection, as others etched eggs, shined shoes, and posed for pictures with Peter Cotton Tail, we spoke back to a storm and saw it "shut-up!"

"Isabel ... Hell!"

The costliest and most deadly hurricane of the 2003 season, Isabel "showed her tail" up and down the east coast! Before making landfall, the city and surrounding areas were placed on high alert. The normal madness followed, leaving empty supermarket and supply store shelves. Every succeeding report dwarfed the last with predictions of life and property loss. Panic struck hard at the heart of anyone who had lived through other storms because no one, in recent memory, could recall the pessimism meteorologist projected this time.

This was "the big one," the "bad mamma jamma," the "mother of all storms:" though this natural disaster was deemed to be anything but nurturing. At an estimated speed of one hundred and sixty five miles, her prelude was enough to advise immediate evacuation and sealed houses. Plywood or duck tape replaced windows in most communities. Neighbors could be seen packing and leaving.

Before we did, we paused to pray, seeking direction for us and directives for those in our care. The response was swift, sure, and stunning. I informed everyone of what I had received. "We were going to weather this storm if we did three things: speak directly to it, release angelic activity to arrest any adversaries, and command shalom to our souls and our property. Also, supplies for home would come in handy, but there would be no loss." Saying the words was hard, since the opposite was playing-out all around us. Each update got worse as local forecasters urged viewers to heed the warnings.

At work, my husband's co-workers were mostly missing or getting off early. Unlike with previous storms, the people left were told to pack all computers and cover all windows. When a co-worker insisted that everyone needed their homes boarded, at least, he became irritated by my husband informing him that ours would be safe. Now we are rational people, unopposed to common sense in such situations, but we had seen God do the incredible so often, we chose to believe He would again. We made that decision for our family, telling everyone else to act in their own best interest (especially members of our congregation). To conclude the stressful conversation, the co-worker remarked, "My grandfather has been here for over fifty years and has never seen a storm of this magnitude miss us!" My husband simply retorted, "I know Someone who is older than your grandfather, and He said nothing was going to happen!"

Bible Study was forthcoming, so we chose to believe God and go. While there, we showed a satellite image of Isabel's course and asked all present to speak what the Lord gave them. In addition, my husband heard a phrase he asked us to repeat, "Isabel, go back to hell!" We probably would have laughed if there wasn't so much at stake. We obeyed, then prayed. Leaving that evening, we "loved-up" on each other, more than usual, and hung around longer. I could only surmise why.

Not ladylike, Isabel made her debut during the day. The afternoon turned dark and dreary right away. My husband decided that the weather was more suited for sleep than for staying up following dismal news reports. Like Jesus, my husband took our son in to nap in the back part of our house. They slept through the downpour. That's all the big one could do, drench the city. By the time she reached our shores, Isabel's strength had waned to one hundred and five, then continued to diminish. When my two fellows returned from the "bottom of the boat," we heard the news caster say the storm had passed, but that power was out in our neighborhood. We laughed, heartily, because our power had allowed us to hear what she just said. The weatherman called it luck that Isabel had changed her course. We knew better, though Lucifer shares the same root word. The Master of the seas had told a few of us to tell her where to go!

As I read over what was just written, I realized how incredulous it must be to anyone who has never known, experienced, or considered the possibility. But this was not an attempt to convince, merely to recollect. I choose not to record others in this forum, since they are more of the same. Yes, there are more! Storms were coming, or upon us, and someone wanted to *try* speaking to see if it would work. Time after time, we—all of us—were witnesses to God doing us a favor.

To the aforementioned I would have added what happened at Carowinds, on the way to Busch Gardens, in Hugh MacRae Park, and before the Birthday Bash at the Beach. In each case, the weather denied us permission to play, but we *attempted* to *act* like Jesus, rebuking the storm. In every instance, there were sudden shifts in the storm. Concerning Hugh MacRae, as soon as the men loaded the last thing we had outside, the clouds gave way, dropping a deluge. It rained the remainder of the day. We didn't even get wet!

CHAPTER 20

"Perfecting Praise"

DURING THE SERVICES of times gone by, the pastor would call his mother up to render a selection before he ministered the word of God. Knowing better than to be disrespectful, you grinned towards your friend and sat towards the edge of your seat. This was bound to be something you'd laugh about for years to come.

You'd endured enough renditions to know the routine: she'd act surprised, then be coaxed from her usual seat with a few, "Sing, Mother…Let Him have His way!" She'd stand up, slowly, then move slower towards the microphone stand on the floor before the podium. After giving honor to God, pastor, saints, and friends, she'd attempt to adjust the mic to no avail. The nearest deacon would assist while she thought of what she'd bless you all with this time.

Now set, she'd nod at the musician to signal her readiness, giving him enough time to hit multiple keys to get to hers. The key would have to be changed mid-song, anyway, because she seldom sang in one. Next, she'd clear her throat, close her eyes, and begin to bellow. "There's not a friend like the lowly Jesus. No, not one. No, not one."

Her voice was squeaky and shaky. You wanted to laugh, but the pastor was facing you, so you'd stand instead, to show your support. Your friends would stand, too, trying to keep from laughing out loud. Mother became louder and more comfortable. Together, you and your cohorts made a silent pact to "help Mother out" by adding "Alright!" or "Let Him use ya!"

But she didn't need your pretense, this was real for her. What she had was better than all the gifts and talents in the room. She had the anointing. So while you were busy playing games, she was making connection. Now you waved, not out of obligation, but conviction. That sorry lil' song had struck just the right note.

People began to sob, sing along, surrender. She had gotten God's attention, so He came to sit in the house her praise built.

At the moment the B-3 Hammond was removed from our old church, we knew we would have to come up with new ways to praise. To compensate, my husband took to the keyboard, learning a few "shout" cords—*just in case*—and a couple of worship songs. Later, I had a hand at it, leaving him to lead praise and worship. It was known that the old minister of music was extremely talented, and that old members were gifted singers. But anyone joining us back then had to be coming for much more than music. We were an assorted assembly, attempting to make up in sincerity what we lacked in performance.

From childhood, most churches I attended had exceptional music. In my church, I led Testimony Service; we didn't call it praise and worship back then. I have grown up with singers and musicians who would work professionally in their lifetimes. If I mentioned names, you would know them all because their careers are still vibrant. On occasions, the group I was a part of recorded gospel albums and sang before packed audiences. During any given rehearsal, convocation, or gathering there was more than ample musical talent to go around. One organist would slide-in as another slid-out of the seat to share their skills. Some were so adept that they could leave one instrument and go to *any* other. Singers in our circles would strive for the soloist spot, and selecting *one* was difficult. So I knew what good music *should* sound like, and we didn't have that.

Although I knew the sound of music, I would have to learn the substance of worship from Faith Deliverance Christian Center in Norfolk, Virginia. There, a small sister named Sharon Riley was one of the best worship leaders I'd ever heard. Her extraordinary abilities were apparent; she could sing and play organ in a way that caused the hairs on your arm to stand at attention. I had never seen her "miss."

Anyone who sat in her worship space was both captivated and catapulted to another dimension. I was intrigued with her as soon as I saw her because she was different from most praise leaders. She refused competition and accepted no accolades. She was not boisterous or braggadocios. Many musicians are. Mostly silent, sparing no unnecessary words, she let it all out with her praise. I admired her even more when I learned that she had honed her skills while traveling with her evangelist mother as a young lady. City after city, service after service, she sang and played every day for two years, with the exception of Christmas. That fact fascinated me, providing the foundation of her solid faith.

Now at Faith, she was the minister of music who was not paid, though her value was immeasurable. I looked forward to praise and worship at Faith Deliverance because I knew I could trust the God in her. She had been with Him, and He would honor their scheduled appointment. We just accompanied her, receiving the lollipop at the end of the visit.

I had been well acquainted with enough musicians to know that Riley was a rare breed, so I set out to be a student, not just a spectator. She presented praise and worship as a goal, not a given. We were taught that there was an objective, and that we were not successful unless we had met it. The Object of our affection was to be sought after until we touched Him, and He touched us. There was a method to ascertain; thank God for anything and everything, praise with all your might, and stay in the glory cloud until *He* is satisfied with worship! "Stand in the glory!" she would encourage.

I took my "studies" very seriously, practicing at home what I was learning at church. The homework helped me pass the test I would have to take later. I am forever grateful for what I learned on my feet, on my knees, or on my face in the classroom of the most proficient praise teacher, Sharon S. Riley.

The subject would have to be tweaked to fit the church I came to pastor. None of the normal elements for praise and worship existed. There were no instruments to speak of and no one to play them. There were no ministers of music, few singers, and fewer leads. Our dynamic was distinct, so the only sound that mattered would have to come from above our heads. Those from an instrument or vocal chords could not always be trusted.

Churches count on music to draw people or keep them coming back. One problem with that is whatever draws them has to be maintained. Anything less could cause anarchy. So even if music got them to come, something else would have to keep them. Most pastors rely greatly on the right sound to support what they have to do next. For me, that sound had to be sanctified, or it was a poor substitute. We had to do something unique to our circumstances. We didn't have the things that music ministry usually requires, so we had to find the thing that would always work for us.

In smaller cities musicians are worth their weight in salary, and they know it. They sell their gifts to the highest bidder or hold the church hostage when they do not get their way. In many instances, the choir or ensemble becomes the musician's own little church, threatening to boycott if their demands are not met. We refused to sell our souls and promptly removed any sign from our front yard. When musicians opened their dialogue with their price, we dismissed the idea of them. One person who played for us mentioned that other churches were contending for her gift with money. Sweetly, we suggested she "take the deal," if that was her main motivation.

I am hurt for pastors who feel obligated to replace relationship with showmanship. They have ministers of music or praise leaders who come late, leave early, and have to put them on their itineraries. Most are praise leaders who won't praise, themselves. Many are not students of the word, and could care less about the message. To them, music is king, so they are just tolerating the sermon until time for them to do their thing. By virtue of their gift, they often have to fight *not* to be arrogant, boastful, or proud. A humble *and* holy musician is a combination hard to find. Those who care less about holiness are a tightly-knit band who stick together, so when you offend one musician, you just may not have music for the revival.

Pastors have their own issues in this regard. Sometimes they can be selfish and insecure, refusing to share their time and space. Some are paranoid, threatened by anyone who acquires applause. Others are unreasonable, seeing even a vacation as abandoning the vision. Sadder, some see the person responsible for the music as their personal attendants, duty bound to serve them, not Him. The most important part of service is not the music or the message, but God.

The Lord designed the sung word and the spoken word to co-exist. Neither music nor the message is the most important thing; the presence of God is. A pastor and a singer/musician should be on the same accord, ushering in the same sound from Heaven. When they are, the rushing mighty wind easily fills the house. But far too many are in adversarial relationships or constantly bumping heads. It is a deliberate distraction of the enemy to keep the service at a surface level. So we meet, week in and week out, but The Dove is not released to transform. Everyone remains the same, and God is kept at the door, knocking. At the Revelation church of Laodicea, Jesus stands without while they keep "having church." How did *He* get outside the church *He* started at Pentecost? Perhaps there came another sound... an alternative.

Whatever we conclude about Satan, we must include the fact that he *is* a musician. Notice I said *is*. Nothing in Scripture remotely suggests that he lost his musical ability, just his accessibility and availability. He used to be the minister of music in Heaven. And not only could he sing and play, the Bible shares with us that he had music built into him. That would be like walking around with pipe organs in your belly! Anyone like that doesn't decide to sing, they can't help but sing. It is who they are, first. It is what they do, second.

Music is where he is most comfortable: his domain. In dark places, he enables, encourages, and embodies sound and song. He does not care who he uses: adult or child, saint or sinner, innocent or ignorant. He just wants them to make music. He knows, well, that music is spirit and can invade space without permission. That is why we remember songs we never set-out to memorize, and why you can recall lyrics from childhood. The current fight for fame and fortune has created a new area of interest for the enemy, even in Gospel and Christian music. If not careful, the longing to be seen and heard can make room for the adversary, who just wants an audience. And he has been at it longer than anyone else.

To Kirk Franklin's, "For those of you who think gospel music has gone too far..." I reply, "Perhaps we have." Maybe we should take a Selah, to see. To make sure we weren't merely making music, our church decided to pause. We chose *not* to have a minister of music, choir, ensemble, or praise leader until further notice. We knew it might keep some people away, but they were the kind we'd rather do without. I love God too much to intentionally hurt Him, and I honor Him too much to allow anyone or anything to poison the presence we *must* have. He was the Only One we needed: everyone or everything else was extra.

Satan is a master of deception, disorder, and delusion. What many churches have is a diluted version of worship, at best. Of course, as a pastor, I was concerned about what the lack of talent might do to our services or the size of the congregation, but I was willing to do without the trappings of "successful" worship rather than keep God away. Because we were not star struck, it became easier and easier to not give glory to visiting singers or musicians. We would not bait them either, requesting their song or skills. When worshipping with us, they would have to bow or stand for our Special Guest like the rest of us. This was His show, His time, His doing; and it was marvelous in our eyes.

Following the lead of the Spirit, we'd begin with prayer, then start singing unto the Lord...with no accompaniment—a cappella. There was nothing to mask our motives. Later, we would seek out vessels of honor who were not singing for the next "hit." They were few and far between, but we managed to collect the music of godly men and women who directed their songs to God and worshipped in place of performance. What we most desired was not inspiration, but intimacy. The former is good for exercise: the latter good for exchange. The likes of Shekinah Glory, Tasha Cobbs, and William McDowell were helpful in leading us to our praise place.

These were not people who visited our church. We humbled ourselves and used their CD's as we told musicians, "no thank you." That's right, our music was *pre-recorded*! No rehearsals were warranted, no choir wars fought, and no flesh was on display. The work was done for us, so all our focus was on doing worship well. Authentic anointing cannot be assembled. It comes already complete. The more we encountered the real thing, the less impressed we became with counterfeits. We now know to thank God by saying it, do something when we praise, and wait in worship until He is content.

A few Sundays ago, God provided another aspect of the multi-faceted worship experience. As I stood on the back row, with eyes closed and hands raised, I had an arresting thought. Since it followed the line of what we were engaged in, I followed along. Initially, I contemplated how much I look forward to this time because it encompasses and encourages song and dance. I appreciate both. With that thought, I continued, "*But, what does someone who doesn't like either get out of this*?" That's as far as I got, when the last song suggested it was time for exaltation.

Up front, I launched into the deep by sharing my incomplete question with the congregants. They looked as puzzled as I must have sounded, awaiting the answer. Well, I didn't have one, but I have had enough of those "Lord, we're trying to have church here!" moments to trust His leading. Then it flowed: praise and worship is all about God—not us, none of us! Neither singer nor non-singer, dancer nor non-dancer matters, *only Him*! If that is true, all of us are responsible for pleasing the Lord, not ourselves.

I used a fashion-forward young lady in our midst to demonstrate. "If I brought Toia a pair of burnt orange stilettos next week, she'd be really pleased." To the illustration, she began to shuffle her happy feet, providing my proof. Seeing the older, more conventional woman behind her, I added, "But if I brought Sister Annie those same shoes, she would have no reason to rejoice." No sooner had I mentioned her name did she start shaking her head. Point well made.

My obligation, then, is to present a gift that pleases the recipient, not someone else. Not even myself. God was the only One we had to give a gift of worship, a sacrifice of praise. So, at all times, we were to enter with thanksgiving, then give Him what He desires and deserves. The Lord gave us a way to always know if we met the objective: do something during praise and worship that was not just what we enjoy. It might even make us uncomfortable. His joy would be full!

Not long ago, someone new to our ministry commented on wanting some new songs. Citing old songs as one of the reasons she left her former church, I gained perspective. First, weren't all old songs *once* new ones? Second, when I inquired of the Lord,

He shared with me that all new things only satisfy the flesh: cars, homes, shoes, toys, and electronic devices. As with them, we grow bored, wanting the newer, next best thing. Before long, that, too, is discarded because it got old. Such is the nature of self.

Praise and worship are spiritual, not carnal: bringing spirit to Spirit. So the newness of a song is irrelevant, but the need for it to be anointed is imperative. The Scripture admonition to "Sing unto the Lord a new song" is often used, out of context, to justify our desire to move on to the latest thing topping the charts. But a thorough search for the verse's meaning relates the new song being referred to as a prophetic song. That has less to do with studios, harmony, pitch, and tone, than the spontaneous praise that pours from, seemingly, nowhere. A new song is not ungodly, it is simply unnecessary. An old one or a new one should flow from the same fountain.

Our ministry now has a few musicians and psalmists. Worship Arts encompasses song, music, praise dance, mime, step, gospel rap, and sign language. But we all know better! We've experienced worship so glorious we could not stand, having to prostrate before His awesome presence. We "shout" (dance) and shout, run, leap, and sometimes sit silently in awe. We stand to honor the Guest and to inform our flesh, at the outset, that this is not its turn. We have been beyond the veil enough to know when we are only in the courtyard. Praise has been passionate and personal because we are clear that it has *never* been about us. Any shadow of turning might make me blow the dust off an old disc.

It is noteworthy that the Bible speaks of *perfected praise* coming from babies or toddlers, not full grown adults. As much as we've done, as close as we've been, we have not yet *grown up to be children*. Ever seen children praise the Lord when they are allowed to? There is total abandonment. They have not learned to fake, perpetrate a fraud, or work to get the applause of peers. Children, even in the face of their natural father, will do whatever it takes to gain and maintain his attention. Adults are too aware of their surroundings, too busy sharpening their skills.

Practice is important: it just will never insure His presence. Practice doesn't make perfect praise. Prioritizing does. When God

becomes our priority, we praise, perfectly. I didn't want Descending
Dove to rehearse just the rituals of praise until we got stuck, permanently doing nothing. Biblical perfection means maturation, and I
long to have us consistently growing in our adoration and celebration of God, alone. Praise Him!

CHAPTER 21

Love Letter

A WALK TO THE *metal box separating your yard from the street was well worth any wait. Tucked between a myriad of bills and bulk lay a simple, single envelope. The scent trailed the walkway, and artistic hugs and kisses made your pace swift in anticipation of its content. You recognized the writing, so the return address forced your heart to skip. You've got mail!*

And from college—you sat in their dorm room; the war—your prayed in their trenches; the new neighborhood—you toured their house; prison—you felt confined in their cell; summer camp—you toasted marshmallows by their fire; Aunt Essie's— you "heard" Uncle Jo snoring; or across town—you couldn't believe it rained on the south side but not the north.

There was something so personal and so permanent about the piece of paper that poured its word into your life. The time taken to remember you and the effort to escort you to their world was no light thing, causing your emotions to heave and sway. Sometimes you read them through veils of tears, and other times you laughed until you were out of breath. Often you fell asleep with them under pillow, only to awaken in the night to reread the parts you wanted never to forget. But you knew you might.

So there—under the bed, in the back of the closet, up in the attic, or over the armoire—is a stack of tear-stained, smell-faded, time-tested envelopes. They remind you of life, love, and lessons learned from the lines of a letter.

The art of letter writing is not practiced much today, as our pace has picked up and our time tripled by technology. From telegrams and facsimiles to emails and text messages, the method has changed, so we have been forced to adapt. There is limited time to put pen to paper and less time to exit our world to enter that of a pen pal. Most writing today is for information, solicitation, or complaint. But just the "other day" letters didn't just tell us something, they gave us something, someone—missed

mamas and distant dads, secret lovers and classmates, sorority
sisters and home boys. So long after pen and paper "kissed," we
kept in hidden places the words of those we could no longer hear
or hold.

I WONDER WHAT SHORTCOMINGS our lives would have without
the timeless letters of Paul the Apostle. How would our churches
handle protocol or etiquette? Would any husband just come up
with the idea of loving his own wife as Christ loved the church?
Would anyone know how much Christ *does* love the church? What
parent would ever think twice about provoking their children to
anger? Not my mama! Not me! When would we look up, expecting
Jesus to come down? Who among us would think that our lives are
being "read" by those who watch us daily? It is Paul's letters that
reveal the Father's heart and how we can fill it.

Writers who placed a letter in a bottle and cast it forth upon
parting waters hoped that someday, one would be retrieved.
Reasoning thus, Jesus advised us not to cast anything of value before
pigs (*or people who wallow*) since they are *incapable* of appreciation.
Instead, He instructed us to put treasured things upon the water,
fully expecting them to return not long after departing. Once, our
ministry sent a single letter out, and received an invaluable return.

It was Valentine's Day. On the university campus we seized the
day to share some real love with those seeking it in all the wrong
places. I had written a love letter from God. After rewording and
rewriting, I finally got it worthy enough to speak the sentiment of
the Sender. The plan for delivery was uncomplicated: everyone in
our ministry would take as many letters as desired, distributing
them to as many families, friends, *and foes* as time would permit.
Because I was the inspired writer, everyone was free to add items
of attention or affection; like a rose, candy, or stuffed animal. This
served as our outreach for the month of February.

Now dismissed, the members of our ministry dispersed to various parts of the city. A few people opted to spread love on campus.
I admired that idea, since many students feel loveless on this lovers'
day. I was enthused by the potentiality of the endeavor, especially
when I considered the dejection of so many of my dorm mates

on this day when I attended university. The letter should, at least, lighten their hearts, I reckoned. After making it my business to select exquisitely decorative paper with matching envelopes, our congregation spoke a blessing over them and included an email address for anyone wishing to discuss what it contained.

The enthusiasm of my expectation wore-off as the hours progressed. Periodic checks of our email failed to prove that anyone was blessed, encouraged, or requested prayer. I cleaved to the belief that I was anointed to pen the prose, and soothed myself with the reminder that I had been obedient. Even the parabolic Word within a letter carried the promise that it would not return void or without accomplishment. That evening, I enjoyed my own Valentine surprises courtesy of the two men I love most.

We had given out many letters that Valentine, but only one reply came back, and it was worth all the rest. Via email, a man made contact with our ministry because he felt obliged to inform us that the labor was not in vain. On the day of our outreach, he, a father, was visiting his son at school. Deciding to take a walk around campus to talk, a child handed his son one of our letters, adding "Jesus loves you" as they parted. The father and his son paused to peruse their Valentine's gift. By the letter's end, both were astonished.

You see, Valentine is not, ordinarily, a parent visiting day. This father made a special trip to see his son out of care and concern. A recent conversation between them revealed that the son, who was sent to school as a Christian, had hit a hard place and was questioning what he'd been reared to believe. His quandary included the reality of God and His love for him. Sensing his son's struggle, this busy father ceased all activities to pay his son an immediate visit. He'd hoped to encourage him and spent that afternoon assuring him of God's love. Into their discussion comes a little child with the confirmation they could use: the love letter.

I read his letter with watered eyes. I thought of the challenges college life presented to *my* faith. I thought of how my mother must have been concerned about my rearing withstanding secular scrutiny. I thought of what more we could instill that would firm our own son's foundation. I was proud of God for not letting this man's son down. It arrested my anxieties about the children of our church who have so much life ahead. I knew that even if God had to send a courier, He could get a word to them just when they need it most.

My husband and I responded to the father's email. It would not be our last exchange. Not long ago, the father emailed again to remind us that they had not forgotten about us. We can never forget them. He wanted us to know that his son had successfully completed his studies at that university and graduated. His faith was still firm.

In another email, he requested prayer for his son, who was being tested for a serious medical malady. To follow-up, he shared that tests came back normal, and his son was well. In addition, the former student was days away from traveling overseas to do missions work. God is awesome! The most recent email asked our permission to print the letter *he still has* in a book he is writing. I granted it, honorably. We keep in touch. Though we have never seen the other's face or heard the other's voice, words on a piece of paper brought us into our worlds. A single love letter went from God's heart, through my hands, to help a father, holding a son, who is now taking that love *to the world*! Below, I have cast that letter upon these waters:

February 14, 2010

Someone Special,

I know you are surprised to receive this. It is given at a time when most people who seek for love hope to find it hidden within heart shaped card board, or dripping from red velvet petals. Many will accept the bait and awaken to an empty pillow beside them the morning after. Some will long for it in the sparkle and splendor of gem or jewel, believing that the planned proposal marked the beginning of ever after.

But the day will come and go without much real exposure to, or many truly experiencing, unfailing loves. The kind I have for you. Yes, you! You: the unique. You: the gifted. You: the greatest expression of my heart's desire.

It seemed better to write it, though I have made many attempts to display it. I've signed it across the sky, whistled it in the wind, and sprinkled it in designer snowflakes. Sometimes you would simply smile, but you still didn't realize it came from me.

I have seen your concealed tears and heard your silent shouts. Concerns about your family, cares about your friends, and uncertainties about the future you have yet to live can hold the heart hostage. I know. Mine had been pierced so badly, it bled. Nothing hurts so deeply as the pain from people you "love to death." But true love always lives again!

I love you eternally. Nothing and no one can change that. Your eyes haven't seen all that I desire to give you, and your ears haven't heard all that I wish to convey. I look forward to sharing. I know how busy you are, but try to "call" as soon as you are available.

Always,

St. John Three Sixteen

P.S. Rest well tonight. I have to work, so I'll be up!

The following Biblical references confirm the veracity of this letter and serves as its inspiration:

- Psalms 19:1
- St. John 19:31–37
- St. John 15:13/Romans 5:8
- Proverbs 10:12
- St. John 14:1, 27
- Jeremiah 31:3
- Romans 8:38, 39
- I Corinthians 2:9
- Jeremiah 33:3
- St. John 3:16

Happy Valentine's Day!

CHAPTER 22

They That Dream

DESCENDING DOVE HAD more dreams than bank deposits. Most ministries do. My bishop's statement, "We may be poor, but we've got class," speaks to a church's polished presentation, but lack of provision. We didn't want to concur with that comparison, but fought to live it down. A pastor must be two things by nature: a visionary and a missionary. Both require money. It is difficult to recreate a vision or accomplish a mission without financial stability. For many years, we strained to provide quality church or render quality programs with little, to no, money. So we've mastered the art of making due.

Following most events guests over-complimented us for things we knew were nothing shy of miraculous. Sometimes we would be counting crumbled-up dollars and adding change in one room while a good time was being had by all next door. The day before most special occurrences found us running around borrowing "the spoils of the Egyptians" to decorate or compensate. But we had to return ours. During a recent church celebration, some of us chuckled at the rants and raves relative to our table settings. A few of us had been out to the beach hours earlier attempting to accommodate the nature-inspired theme we were *forced* to use. Designers and party planners give high marks for our decorum. That's always been funny to those of us who bargain shopped for almost everything and weren't too proud to beg for others.

We piecemealed costumes, used furniture from home, and cooked for our own catered affairs. We created all stationary and designed all advertisements. When families could not afford weddings and funerals, we did the programs, planning, prepping, praying, preaching, and participating. Openhanded, we've given gifts and surprises for all occasions. I still can't explain *how*. Our ministry has been faithful over less than a *few* things.

In the beginning we had nothing to speak of but each other. Later, we learned more, so we did more. Over the years we've been blessed with new cars, new homes, and new members, but at times, the same old nemesis would make an appearance. And although grateful to be rid of "never enough," his twin "just enough" is no friend either. There was simply just not enough to realize the dreams we were sure wasn't pizza from the night before.

God kept giving me stuff: creative ideas and images so clear I could almost touch them. Some God-inspired ideas were hard to ignore because in my dreams they were already done. In rapid succession, I'd have one creative impulse after another. Things were truly trying for me, too, because He blessed me with vivid vision. I'd see things in techno-color and high-definition that I believed we were supposed to do, but hadn't a clue how we might do them.

As a small child growing up with meager means, my ongoing desire was for someone to knock on any of the many doors we had and simply tell us *how* to get out. As a grown pastor, I saw what our church could be, but not how to make those dreams come to fruition. I didn't want to "spin around again, touch three more people, or high-five another neighbor," as was often done at meetings." We needed information! Inspiration was our gifting. But where were the people with the foresight and insight who weren't taking the little we had to show us how they acquired what they have? Maybe we were about to meet.

Nothing of noteworthiness seemed to mark the day. It was typical in almost every way. I went about my regular routine, thankfully. I have learned to value the blessing of normality: the emergency that didn't happen, the crisis that didn't demand attention. I roused the fellows, prayed, dressed, ate a quick breakfast, took our son to school, and began work on that evening's class.

About midday, I had the strangest impulse to stop what I was doing and pray. Now steeped in books and papers, I continued, intending to pray in a minute. There it was again. I was so close to being done, but now had a hard time concentrating. So I stopped. A yearning to pray in the Spirit came next. Sitting in what I call the prayer chair, I prayed until my spirit rested. I don't know what I said, and I didn't know why I said it. I'd addressed the Father in the authority of His Son, trusting whatever was worth the interruption was accomplished. I returned to my work. One reason the

Bible gives for praying in the Spirit is to build up oneself. I would require edification.

Within hours, a text message requested a call. Someone had contacted our administrator and wanted to speak with my husband and me, together. Acquainted with the people, we deemed that there must have been something of importance for them to make such an effort. On a break from his job, my husband and I called the couple. They were pleasant to us when our paths crossed, and we shared polite greetings but had no daily dealings with them. Now on three-way, we made casual courtesies then readied to hear them. Theirs was a direct question: "Do ya'll have a church, yet?" one of them started.

"Not yet," one of us replied.

"Do you have something in mind?" one of them uttered.

"As a matter of fact, we do," one of us answered.

"Well, how much money do ya'll need?" someone from their end continued.

This is already one of the best conversations of my life!" I thought.

From our end, my husband picked up the dialogue. He told them the current asking price of a building we had been looking at for years. When they interjected that we might require more and spoke of the amount someone was willing to let us have, I dropped the telephone, hollered, and ran around my house in circles! Remembering my manners, I did return to say that I needed a moment to process, but my husband would continue to talk. I was so overcome! While celebrating, a thought occurred to me: the Holy Spirit had refused to "let me alone," earlier.

When I was calmer and capable of conversation, my husband explained all the details. We were invited to hear the particulars via conference call the next evening. We were ready. Speakers on and pad prepared, we sat attentively. The moderator welcomed varied guests. Right away, I realized this was an interesting assembly by the multiple accents and areas they were calling from. There were many in attendance, taking a while to work through the roll call. Each salutation was one I could identify from my church background. These people sounded like believers. Periodically, we were informed that the host would join us momentarily. The couple who called us earlier had given the name, but we were surprised when *she* finally came on the line. We both assumed the person would be male. Sexism is still subtle, sly.

Her voice was unique, clear, and controlled. I tried to distinguish ethnicity, but it was difficult. Interestingly, she sounded black *and* white. I would have guessed she was born in another part of the world or had traveled abroad. I could tell she was older, and the younger voices paid homage to her. The multiple men and women on the line apparently respected her, honoring the position in their introductions.

After greeting, she got right to the business at hand. "Since childhood," she started, "I have had a recurring dream." In specific detail, and with certainty, she directed the majority of her communication to any newcomers. From that, I gathered that most of the people present this night were accustomed to what she would articulate. Simply stated, she believed that she was born to bring abundance to the body of Christ. So fully assured was she that most of her years had been spent finding, gathering, and disseminating information relative to business and finance. A business professional, she and a group of other likeminded entrepreneurs had covenanted to be conduits of wealth transfer to the parts of His body that most needed attention. Together, they had pooled their resources to find ways and means to make her dream a reality for others.

They introduced themselves as a Christian based financial restitution consortium. They had been meeting and planning for years. The leader mentioned having invested everything and its leadership made substantial contributions. The older members, I believed, would bring necessary prudence. The younger, I thought, added enough vitality and variance to bring balance. Youthful strength and aged experience seemed to be the hallmark of this conglomerate. By strength, I really am referring to normal physical ability because on any given five-hour, after midnight call, the silver haired saints could outlast most younglings. My husband and I would begin joining the party line, encouraging ourselves by joking that these "oldies, but goodies," had been napping all day, preparing to endure. We, on the other hand, were sleepy!

Not only were there grandpas, grandmas, and grandchildren,

but doctors, attorneys, analysts, accountants, business owners, and financers. That gave me peace relative to some of the information they relayed. From a myriad of backgrounds and cultures, what they seemed to share was a love for God, His people, and His cause. Even when I didn't agree with everything said or done, I believed that they were Kingdom committed.

Years back, after the very first telephone conversation between me and the man I would marry, he sent me a considerate gift. The gesture, to me, spoke to the expanse of his soul. Within months of dating, I asked of his aspirations. When his reply revealed a primary desire to be philanthropic, I was at home. As far back as I could recollect, my greatest longing had been to give. Today, closest family and friends comment that I will give anything away, including things given to me. I try to minimize that. But the truth still remains, God has enlarged the capacity of my heart, and I want to be like Him—giving. To me, it is the highest expression of His love, the One Who *so gave.* Some, who live with financial struggles, fight never to return to them. So they are frugal to a fault, stingy, and often hoard. I believe the Scripture provides another way: give and it shall be given. My husband and I share that sentiment.

We have taught the members of our ministry to be magnanimous. They know that many people are not. So we would have to show our world the Giver in tangible, visible ways. Initially, my husband and I gave away everything to move to North Carolina. While here, we've poured out our time, talent, treasure, and testimony. We trained our child not to hold on to anything and stressed that what is given comes back with interest. *Every* member of our congregation has been the recipient of gifts and good things we wanted to bestow.

Because they had seen our consistent sacrifices, all members knew how to give. To practice the lessons of liberality, we initiated situations that enabled others to glean from our blessings. Many have been on the receiving end of what the Father let us borrow. In our community, at the grocery store, by the gas pump, or on the side of the road, we have created ways to demonstrate Daddy's desire. Someone who has just had their cleaner's bill paid by one of us will often remark, "Why'd you do that?" The simple answer, "Because God loves you so much, He gave."

During the very first finance conference call, I heard that someone wanted to show us how to get out and give with no strings attached. That caused me to dream again. This would be the first of numerous calls and innumerable information. Those old sorted seniors knew more than anyone might give them credit for. There was something else I needed to know, though.

My husband and I were aware of Ponzi schemes, plots, and ploys, so we proceeded with caution. As nice as the group appeared, we began to do our own homework, refused to give them money for what they said was freely offered, and prayed more earnestly for wisdom while we awaited manifestation.

All of this happened some time ago. Patience, I must admit, has not been my best virtue, but for some it has been an enemy. The Bible admonishes us to let patience have its perfect work. The problem with that "Patience girl" is that she takes her time, working on her schedule. Meanwhile, we'd pray for monthly miracles and get them, but I wondered how long it would take the provision to match the vision.

One night while watching television, I saw something I didn't want to see, but needed to. During an episode of "American Greed," I couldn't help but notice that a group of unsuspecting ministers had fallen prey to a charlatan promoting Kingdom finance and promising wealth transfer. Worse, they had given the chameleon money and entrusted this "man of God" to return their investments with interests. Something within me rose and fell! I could not dismiss the similarities, with one notable exception: we had not been requested to give one dime. As sorry as I felt for the men and women who had relied on the ranting of a liar and thief, I was as relieved that there had been no request from us to exchange money.

Not long after that episode, the group we were a part of asked for money. We, respectfully asked to have our names removed from their roster. Many are still meeting and are still sincere. I am in no wise inferring that the conglomerate which instructed us in the Father's business is crooked or calculating. I am, however, suggesting that pastors and members should be sure that we aren't trying to make our own dreams come true, and at any costs!

Descending Dove had already paid the price of admission. And for so long we sat watching the previews of a coming attraction. We dream bold, brazen even. But these are not dreams you can conjure. Dr. Martin Luther King Jr.'s dream, in example, was too mammoth to begin in the mind of a man. The Biblical Joseph's dreams seemed contradictory to everything in his immediate environment. They are the ones which come to you without provocation. No person can make themselves dream! Because God is the One who initiates them, He must, of necessity, be the One to bring them to pass. I'll just keep my eyes wide shut!

In one of my favorite Psalms, 126, Israel rehearsed their struggle. But something had changed. There had been a turn over, and the Lord had been so faithful that it seemed like they were dreaming. Now, they were laughing and singing. Even their enemies had to concede that God had been good to them. They knew it, and were glad about it. But before they experienced overdue joy, there had been overwhelming weeping.

It was November. The dusk was crisp and clear. Exhilaration enveloped our home as we prepared for the Evening of Class. The culmination of fund raising efforts at Faith Academy School of Excellence was always a highlight of the year for anyone who supported Christian education. The school our pastor founded had earned the right to be celebrated.

My husband's fancy duds were draped across our master bed and my dress had, finally, arrived. My godmother found the perfect one for me and sent it. Men certainly like to look good, but dressing up for women is a timeless and time consuming tradition we take seriously.

It began when we were little girls, grinning at the reflection in the mirror. We primped and poked until we got it right. Then, with stolen lipstick and rouge, mama's too big high heels, drooping pearl necklace, dangling clip-on earrings, floppy hat with the flower, and shiny dress from the back of her closet, we prepped before our imaginary photo shoot. The scene would be played out again and again, until we grew to fit those shoes.

With little over an hour to get dressed for the big banquet, I rose from my relaxed position to dress. My hair was the way I liked it for such occasions, and all my accessories were laid out. All I had left to do was slide on the stunning sequin gown with matching sparkly jacket. Because men have so much less to do, the entire upstairs was my domain for the moment. I dropped the dress to the floor and stepped in. Bringing it past my calves, knees, and hips was easy. The rest proved more demanding.

After several failed attempts, I called my husband who commanded all his brute strength and could not raise the dress above my midsection. I sucked in, pushed in and tried to stuff in, but no go. In frustration, I flopped onto the bed to think. The more I thought, the worse the outcome. I began to ball, crying like someone had just socked me in the stomach. I checked the label, maybe it was the wrong size. No, that's not it! The dress was the right size, but, obviously, I wasn't. That realization made me cry more.

My sweet husband sat beside me, carefully choosing his words, "Is there something else you can wear?" But this was the dress I had been looking so forward to getting into. I cried, again. In the middle of my dilemma, I had an epiphany. During my younger, dumber, I-think-I'll-be-a-model phase, I had seen a trick that just might work. "Honey, can you please bring me some duck tape?" I requested. You know duck tape is the must-have essential in every home? So I knew we had some.

Together, he and I worked like engineers to bind anything that was loose (this is still a Christian book)!" In between wraps, he chuckled, but I was all too serious. It worked! That dress zipped, the jacket slipped, and we were off to the event. No one knew our secret, until now.

Funny thing about secrets, they never remain that way. Weeks after that evening, a quick trip to an urgent care revealed mine. I was very pregnant! I cried, again! But these tears were weighted with bliss. I was beside myself! On December 16, 1996, I gave birth to a blessed baby boy. Entering our home a few days before Christmas, I recalled the scene which unfolded months earlier. There we were, tugging, trying to make me stop crying. I had been carrying a precious seed and didn't know it.

The end of Psalm 126 relays that after all that crying and straining, pushing and pulling, Israel would come back, without a doubt, bringing their sheaves (translated: bundle) with them. Like the dream baby boy I gave birth to, Descending Dove would have many babies of its own. And the "baby Daddy" would give us the means to support them all! God is no deadbeat dad.

CHAPTER 23

Building Project

ONLY CERTAIN KIND *of people frequent model homes: guests, serious seekers, and builders. Guests are just people who like to look. They travel from community to community admiring the style, structure, and staging of each. They will sit, listen to the agent, and eat the cookies, but they are just wasting time. Serious seekers are not wasteful, so time is of the essence. The bank has already approved the loan, or they have managed to raise the amount required to acquire their dream. They can see themselves living there, so they will be back—for good.*

The builder is back to inspect the place. Is the work quality? Were the best materials utilized? How will the occupants function in their new space? Do others admire what he has completed?

Our church has had cookie eating guests and those seekers who came back for good. But nothing gets us as stirred as the Builder making a house call. Will we pass His inspection? Is our quality up to His standards? Is our ministry material top-of-the-line? Can anyone tell that all the marks of the Builder are on us? His style and signature are everywhere! We are His workmanship: not the church we are building, the church building we are! Descending Dove has never had a building project. We are the building project!

"Except the Lord build the house, they labor in vain that build it..."
—PSALM 127:1

People who have a church background have their own concept of what it is suppose to be. First, church is supposed to look like one; second, it's supposed to sound like one. Next, the pastor should be male. Our church fits none of the classic stereotypes. For years, we had not been in our own church building; we had no live music, and I, certainly, am not a man. These distinctions proved challenging for many people, and I understood their discomfort. Most people don't like being moved out of their comfort zones.

Our members, in the beginning, had to make major adjustments of their own, since they, too, were traditionally churched in almost every sense of the term. When we met each other, men and women were separate and not so equal, usually seated to suggest the same. Some practices were, frankly, too embarrassing to make mention of. The law was strictly enforced and strictly adhered to.

Once, I gave a woman who shared my birth month a gift. Tearing paper and working her way through the box, her smile weakened. She tried to maintain gratitude, but I knew something was awry. The three-piece ensemble was pretty enough; it was just the wrong color. Red! That hue was associated with *other* kinds of women. I immediately thought of the crimson streams that saved us. But color wasn't the only point of contention. Most of the women also didn't cut their hair, wear women's pants, jewelry (wedding bands excluded) or "paint" their faces. Men never had as much to contend with. Perhaps because they were the "heads:" and often the ones establishing the rules. Almost everyone shied away from certain recreational activities, gatherings with sinners or other religious groups, and like contradictions.

From the start, I didn't get bogged down trying to change any of that. I didn't even set-out to change them. I didn't know how. The first clear directive I received from the Father was "Feed them Jesus." Using the fresh example of my motherhood, He instructed me not to let anyone near the new "baby" because they might be contagious. For the next year, no ministry guest was invited to fellowship with us. We had had enough church. What we needed was new life, not another revival meeting. Nothing dead *there* needed to be brought back to life. No rules, edicts, or judgments could make a difference. They were already so deep in doctrinal mire that He was the only One Who could reach way down and pick them up. All I knew was Jesus—and Him crucified. All I had was Jesus— and what He brought with Him. All I gave was Jesus—and what He wanted us to have. Anything else would have to be built on Him. That foundation is still sure.

The more we saw Christ, the less we saw ourselves. That image set us free! Not free to live like the world, but free to be the salt and light in it. Nothing can be lit when we are our own holiness. The

Gospel, we discovered, cast its own light. It is brighter and lasts longer than the artificial ones we attempt to shine. No building is complete without light, so He added ours.

We were once the humiliated church, embarrassed by a past we had little to nothing to do with. Heads wagged, tongues lashed, and names were called. Members faced indignation and insults from family and friends because they stayed with me. I stayed with God, often wondering when we would live down the systemic sabotage or shame.

To be honest, at first I was somewhat ashamed of the flock that followed me. Because of what they'd survived, some looked sad, struggled emotionally, and lacked polished social skills. A few were uncouth, loud, and obnoxious. A number were stand-offish and delicate. The presumption was that they were from the backwoods, so they must be backwards. Once, someone visited our ministry and hurled comments relative to how "country everyone and every-thing was!" One statement was sufficient to support her premise, but she railed on for way too long. She has not been asked back. I had my own issues to work through regarding the people and the place God put me in, but no one else had the right to deride them. They were now, me. And we would be fine, thank you very much!

On our first visit to the big city, Norfolk, I had to encourage them to mingle and make themselves meet someone new. Reluctantly, most did and still communicate with those "strangers" today. On a similar occasion, we separated our few and forced them to sit at tables with anyone other than someone they came with. Once, we split up our entire ministry and took everyone to dinner at the homes of people they didn't know who were members of our parent church. Everyone returned with tales of triumph and joy, in spite of themselves.

I marvel at pastors who have only to preach good sermons. I had to cover the length and breath of life and godliness. Showing and telling the members how to do what the Bible says we should took one brick at a time. We planned field trips to Golden Corral to practice the skills from our etiquette lessons. Don't laugh, that was a step-up at the time! We transported the entire ministry to view model homes to help them expand their borders. We brought our bills to church and worked through them. We had classes, training, or sessions covering every imaginable life skill (and some you would never conceive). It has all been worth the investment. We were being built-up on every side.

Today, we are not the same! The change has nothing to do with how we look, but what we believe. We are who God says we are, have what He says we can have, and do what He says we can do. We have risen from the dead to announce that Jesus is flaunting the keys. He has turned our mourning into dancing, replaced ashes with beauty. We slip into praise without much effort, though heaviness was once our daily garb. We are no longer orphans, adopted by a Monarch. We are the King's kids, royal and regal. God has taken ruins and made us solid, sturdy, and structurally sound. He has worked us over!

Sometimes, when people get a glimpse of where they *think* God is taking you, they want to tag along. So we've had our share of stragglers. But, a stray will not stay where he is not getting rations. Put him to work, and he will find the next backyard. We are in the house.

What about the swine trio? Those little pork rinds just wanted to build their style of abode and have a few dinner parties. They must have gotten along better than most humans because each planned to show up at the other's event. At the housewarming, they danced, played, and exchanged gifts. Having enjoyed a good old mud bath, they intended to finish off leftovers from the troth deli. But an outside disturbance interrupted their dining pleasure. They thought they heard something, but the howl subsided, so they continued. There is was again. Perhaps the wind was just being unruly. Then it came, the gruff that gave them pause.

"Hey, you burly brothers! Nobody called me for dinner! Somebody open up and let me come in!" the big bad wolf barked. From under the table, one of the pigs panted, then replied, "It's a private affair. So please go away and leave us alone!" The wolf grimaced, "You trying to tell me you don't want me in there?" No pork belly responded. They all knew that he didn't want to

party. He wanted pork chops. "So that's the way it is, huh? Well, I'll let ya'll think about it for a minute while I take a deep breath. But when I count to three, I'm a huffing and a puffing, and that mess you built is coming down!"

The silence was deafening. They huddled together. "Three!" The straw from the farmer's market was no match for the breath of the enemy. That baby brother pig's house toppled, strewn all over the front lawn. When they felt the wind hit their coiled tails, that was all the evidence they needed that the building project failed. It was time to run!

Now, you would gather that such a traumatic incident would make them better builders the second time. You would be wrong. So those sticks found in their uncle's backyard were another bad idea. But, after a second near death experience, the third piggly wiggly decided to fortify his architectural design with time tested brick and mortar.

The confident big bad wolf found out about the dinner-by-invitation-only, and decided to make another appearance. This time there were no greetings wasted. He drew back and blew hard. Nothing! He inhaled and exhaled again. Not a thing! Perhaps he should stop smoking. He discarded the nicotine stick and filled his lungs with as much air as they could hold. But no bullying or bad breath prevailed. No tease, taunt, or threat could tumble the house made with quality materials. And everyone knows you don't put costly craftsmanship on a faulty foundation.

"Therefore whosoever hears these sayings of mine and does them, I will liken him unto a wise man, which built his house upon a rock…"

—St. Matthew 7:24

Told You So

OVER THE YEARS my husband and I have prophesied things that seemed incredulous, even while we spoke them. After some services, we'd sit over dinner saying, "Wow, did you hear what the Lord said?" as if we weren't the ones spoken through. They were so over-the-top or out of our league that speaking such things was more than a leap of faith. They were *laps* of faith around a field we couldn't see. For me, the prophetic tends to begin as some farfetched thought that intensifies, and then refuses to be denied. When I first started getting such nudges, I'd try to keep talking, but my words would begin to seem senseless to me. The prophecies were like commercials, coming in the middle of something already preprogrammed.

As a new pastor, I was petrified at the thought of sounding insane. I also place great weight on truth and shun "freak shows." So all vigilance preceded anything I believed God was saying, in addition to what I had studied and outlined. One of the first things I uttered had to do with a man losing his job, but not missing income. Now this man had been on his job for many years prior to my arrival. He had tenure, benefits, and a good relationship with his boss and co-workers. All of that notwithstanding, he was let go at the beginning of the week following the prophecy and hired with better pay and more benefits before the weekend. Whew! I was sure glad that was God!

Many such prophetic insights would invade our plans over the years. Since Biblical foretelling is always sent to edify, my husband and I were careful to include encouragement, granting great hope and help in time of need. Both gentle rebukes and stern reprimand were accompanied by methods of restoration. The more I saw come to pass, the less uncomfortable I was with calling things one way when they looked the antithesis. Always, God would use His Word to announce what He was about to do. We attempted to record them all, since others might find them outlandish. Often, we would have to review the prophecies concerning us because they seemed so far removed from where we were. Below are the ones we committed to memory and chose to war with over and over again:

- *From the story of Joseph*, someone would be in the same hard place we were. They needed a Word that only we could give them. When received, it possessed the inherent power to liberate them. After returning to a position of influence, they would be reminded of us and affluent others would send for us. Because we were being prepped in private, our public presentation would bring us before great men who would offer us positions of authority. Our families would be the beneficiaries of how the Lord had blessed. The man standing behind that open door was our Butler.

- *From the story of Ruth*, God would assign someone to us, to whom we were loyal. Following our Naomi's lead, we would obey specific instructions of how we were to glean. That obedience would cause us to win the affection and attention of the right Person. We needed only to please Him. For doing so, He would give us extra, make us forget our loss, and intercede on our behalf. We would covenant with Him and our lineage would be blessed.

- *From the Gospel of Luke,* there would be ministering women, whose desire and determination were selfless. They had suffered themselves, but pulled together to obtain the objective. They were not lazy, rising early to seek Him, bringing the best they possessed. Before, they had ministered to Jesus of their substance (Chapter 8:1–3). This day, their anointing was to care for His body (Chapter 24:1–10). God promised us Marys, Joannas, and Susannas whose primary concern was to help take care of us, members of His body, so that we could minister to others.

- *From the Gospels,* God shared with us that Josephs and Nicodemus' would work in concert to carry us. They would be connected to the proper authorities to attain favor. From positions of business and policy they would seek to effect change, since they had been changed by their encounters with the living Christ. By the grace on them, they would be shown greater grace and allowed to take us where no one else could.

- From the Epistles and the Gospel of St. Luke, the Lord invited us to "help ourselves!" He reminded us that *all* of His grace is abounding towards us and that we have *all* sufficiency in *all* things, abounding to every good work. He caused us to recall that we have been granted *all* things that pertain to life and god-liness. He reemphasized that we could rest in all He provided, because it is His good pleasure to give us His kingdom, not just heaven. That was a Word worth waiting for!

Most of the aforementioned was spoken many years ago. We have fought with them at times we felt defeated. We have believed them, confessed them, and reminded each other of them while battles raged. As of this writing, we have met all those shadows and types, receiving from each: our Butler, Naomi/Boaz, Ministering Women, and Managerial Men. God has performed so many viable, verifi-able miracles that this writing cannot contain them all. Prophecies have been bodacious and veracious, lived out before our eyes. In addition, God prepared a table big enough for us to help ourselves and sent out invitations.

CHAPTER 25

Pumps in the Pulpit

GOT TO LOVE *those insecure sisters! They were never the prettiest or the brightest." They couldn't cook or clean. And they were, obviously, repulsed by the cinders in the fireplace. That may be why we don't remember their names. Those menial, mundane tasks were left up to their stepsister, Cinderella. The refusal to take on even common household chores would work to their disadvantage. Slothfulness is nobody's friend. Regardless of how charming a girl can be, no man wants someone who is just fluff. All they had to offer was a glitzy dress and batting eyes, and that would only last the length of the ball.*

"Cindy" had her own issues, too. After the death of her dad, she was forced to try to fit in with the likes of a detestable stepmother and her envious daughters. Nevertheless, she was given the benefit of attending the ball, in secret, and won the affection of the king's son. That's all well and good, but the issue is time sensitive. She has to accomplish her objectives within a relatively short period. At the stroke of twelve a.m., there would be midnight madness if she hadn't achieved the desired results. So caught up was she that the bongs from the time keeper jolted her from jubilation, dictating an abrupt exit. In haste, her borrowed glass slipper slid off and rested on the pavement behind the carriage

(I know this story too well).

Having clearly not fit the bevy of beauties that had been summoned to his ball, the son set out to search for the one. In his possession was the only piece of forensic evidence he needed to find her: the shoe. It was rare, exceptional, distinct from any he'd ever seen, and tailor made to fit only one foot in the entire kingdom.

At the home of Cinderella, the overconfident stepmother pushed her daughters to the front of the line to see if either would be wed to royalty. If one failed, surely the other could be

crowned. Despite attempts to squeeze and stuff, something was
out of sorts, and no duck tape could fix it. "Dem feets" were just
too big or bulky, flat or funky, calloused or crusty. But he was
out of houses, so surely someone had been overlooked. Forced
to the forefront, Cindy is made to try on the slipper designed for
her in the first place. No wonder it fit!

When I first began to preach, it was apparent right away that I
didn't *fit in* well anywhere. First, I was born a woman, not a man
trapped in a woman's body. I am a girly girl at that. I like to be
prissy and primp. I like Prada and pretty things. I fuss over my hair,
check my clothes until I walk out the door, and have a soft spot for
shoes. I appreciate natural hair, but weave will do. I enjoy shopping
for myself and almost anyone else. I arch my eyebrows and shave
my legs. I believe that looking your best is the gift you give yourself
(my husband will contest). I prefer my nails and furniture polished.
I want the food I cook to look and taste good. I abhor dust, dirt, or
disorder. I can do without shallow conversation, preferring deeper
discussions. I see burps, belches, grunts, or any other general body
sounds guys make for fun as gross. *Yulk!* Give me glamour and
glitz. Wrap me in a throw with sweet flavored tea and a long, good
novel. I enjoy being a girl. Preaching did not refuse me that favor.

To make things more interesting, God transitioned me from
preacher to pastor. Did God forget *women weren't supposed to do*
that? Just when men were warming up to the idea of having me
share the pulpit on Women's Days, God flipped the script, assigning
me a permanent seat *beside them*. Most didn't like it. Many would
never accept it. Some, conveniently, forgot to invite me, or spoke to
every other pastor in the room when I was present. Others were in
denial, resigning themselves to address me only as Angel or Sister.
But the title *Pastor* often got stuck in their throats. While they took
another swallow, I stepped into a new pair of shoes.

In the same way I worked to fit that fabulous evening gown, I
have made many attempts to reshape myself for my surroundings. Perhaps if I tried to act like pastors I knew, I could do what
they did. But the forced fit always failed. The more music mingled
with my message, the harder the Word was to retain. Cultural and

entertaining, the concept of an organ backing up a preacher can be confusing. The sound seems to make some listeners tune you out. The more saved I tried to look, the less effective my witness. The more I tried to fill the shoes of the man I came after, the less people came to church. Walking a mile in everyone's shoes was causing me to walk backwards. I had to find *my size,* and then start walking forward.

The first thing I did was calm down and teach. Charisma and clarity had to meet in the middle. Systematic Bible Study provided a solid foundation to stand on. When I noticed that the majority of our congregation was young and most didn't even own a suit, I came out of mine. And when I discovered that ministry comes from the Holy Spirit, not masculinity or femininity, my soul calmed down. No man or woman is capable of bringing conviction or redemption. That is a pious, prideful notion. Salvation is spiritual, *wrought by God* through available vessels, so they can be male or female. My shoes were beginning to feel better as I walked around in them.

But no one keeps their shoes on. When feet begin to ache or grow tired, we kick them off. Attention, then, needs to be given to the less comely part of the body. God is teaching me to pause when needed and pace myself for the long haul. This is not a sprint, it's a marathon. The Bibles states that people who preach the Gospel have beautiful feet. The woman I am appreciates the analogy. I have had enough pedicures to know that they are not *as* beautiful without rest. After time and care, you slide back into your shoes, continuing the journey.

I have worn many shoes during our travels, and it's just as well; I've never met a woman who doesn't like them. I have had to fill many rolls, play many positions, and wear many hats to match my footwear. To that, I find a supply for the children of Israel very surprising:

> "...I have led you forty years in the wilderness: your clothes have not gotten old on you, and your *shoe has not gotten old* on your foot."
>
> —DEUTERONOMY 29:5

"Your clothes did not get old on you; neither did your *foot swell*,
    these forty years."
                                                —DEUTERONOMY 8:4

Not only would there be no need for food from a supermarket,
water from a faucet, or an outfit from the mall, God would make
their shoes endure the harsh conditions of the wilderness. As former
slaves, I wondered if they were already adept at making their own
shoes. In Egypt, there would have been no income to supply this
necessity. Why did God include such a provision? I believe it's because
He wanted them to know He was in this with them, handling every
minute detail, concerned about even swollen ankles. He was walking
them through the wilderness, always steps ahead.

He had to go before me, too. When I first became a "lady preacher,"
no one who sincerely loved me could step inside my shoes. I had
been walked to the precipice, but needed to take further steps alone,
by faith. My feet had gotten wet, been tired, and ached. But I saw
stretches of road still ahead, and all I knew to do was put one foot
in front of the other, stepping in His footsteps.

I have walked many miles, especially as we moved from place to
place. I have had to limp, drag, and be pulled. When I could not
run, I walked, or crawled. What I am most grateful for is that He
whose Spirit moved upon the face of the waters kept me moving. The
pumps I wore when I first preached in the pulpit of the small North
Carolina sanctuary, I still own. I have not outgrown them, though I
have grown up in ways I didn't know I had to.

My pastor instructs us to preach in our ministry context. "You
were born an original," she says. "Don't die a copy." I was *born*
a woman. I was *born again* to preach. The context the Lord outlined for me to fulfill this calling cannot conform to anyone I know.
During a recent conference, my pastor made mention of a revelation that rested in me. After all these years, she now knows that
she has attempted to fit the Kinston fellowship into the mode of
her previous ministry. At a time of contemplative introspection, the
Lord comforted her with the realization that "this is not a church.
This is a mission. Stop trying to fit the prescribed pattern: and do
what I have given you all the components to do."

I'm not sure if anyone in the room was as liberated as my husband

and I following those words. Our feet got light! We returned to Wilmington with renewed strength, teeming with hope. We had cleaved to the idea that if we tried to make it work long enough, *it just would*. But if something doesn't fit, you must fall back, at some point, and ask why. The answer was supplied with our pastor's reveal.

We *are* a church, but the practices and presentations the Lord placed inside of us extend beyond the four walls. We are dramatic and demonstrative, with an uncommon way to share the Gospel. God was saying that we were free to step in time with *Him*, doing things *His* way. We could do the talk show format, put the chairs in a circle, use Sundays for outreach, celebrate in a movie theater, and turn the entire sanctuary into an airplane, if we wanted to. As long as we kept the first thing first, no step would be taken alone.

There are shoes you wear around the house and others made for anything you do outside your doors: shoes for walking, running, dancing, and jumping. There are work shoes and shoes you play in. Clogs, platforms, galoshes, flats, heels, loafers, sneakers, crocks, boats, sandals, boots, and pumps: shoes are available for any sport you fancy, even snorkeling. Baseball, football, and soccer players use cleats for their feet. One pair of my shoes was for home and family, another for church, another for serving, and another for playing. I like them all.

You can tell a lot about a person based on what shoes they choose to wear: conservative, classy, sassy, seductive, posh, plain, or poor. Not having shoes or deciding not to wear any speaks to something else entirely: *lack*—wish I could, or *liberty*—don't want to. I am not the walking around barefoot type, but I only wear shoes I am free to be myself in.

Because I wasn't reared with a silver spoon in my mouth, my mother had to make the most of bare necessities. Most of the time, my siblings and I wore clothes and shoes given to us by others who were fortunate enough to be purchasing something new. Their old, new to us, hand-me-downs were then handed down to the next one of us when the biggest had outgrown them. On rare occasions, mama would get some "extra change" which meant we could get something from a real store. (Once I had a pair of tennis shoes from a grocery store. No joke!) At such times, since I was "getting to be a big girl," mama would spring for some new shoes.

The day of shopping would find me barely able to contain my excitement. Inside the shoe department, the man with the measuring tape would have to size me because they said I was growing like a weed. I wasn't quite sure what that meant, but everyone smiled when they said it, so I did too. My smirk actually had more to do with the pleasure of being present for this special event. I'd slide out of my left shoe (since the man said they differed in size) into the too cold metal apparatus on the floor in front of the wooden chair. Saying the size often elicited a sigh from mama, who always managed to be astonished. I wanted her to go back to smiling about the weed growth. Since she was committed, we could move on to the best part.

Picking out a pair wasn't without its complications. There were so many to select from and these must last me until the next far away time. Row upon row, stack after stack, we'd hunt for the transformed cow. My mother liked real leather, she said, "because it had longevity." This really meant: "Lord, let her be able to wear these 'til the next bonus." She and I seldom saw eye to eye on the right shoes: heel too high, price too high, too wild, too womanly. When we finally arrived at the pair she would have chosen without me, they were perfect. I was just glad to be the recipient of my own pair.

At that point my mother always did something I considered peculiar. She'd signal the salesman and instruct him to reach the box labeled size six on the side. He seemed to be in on her little secret, but I was baffled. I clearly heard the man say that I was a size five, so why were they both feigning that a larger size was correct? Perhaps there was something about shoe buying I didn't comprehend. I knew better than to question grown folks' sanity, and I wouldn't dare chance messing up this propitious occasion.

On our way out of the store, I prepared to question the woman who held her head in confidence. Before asking, I had enough good home training to preface my statement: "Thanks, Mama, for my pretty new shoes. I really appreciate it." If she had any reservations about spending the money, they subsided with my gratitude.

"You're so welcome, baby." She said smiling.

Letting that soak, I continued, "Hey, mama. Can I ask you something?"

"Sure you can, baby?" she invited.

"Why did you buy my shoes a size bigger?" I ventured.

"Your feet are growing so fast, that you need space to stretch them out," She offered. "So I buy a bigger pair of shoes just to give you time to grow into them."

"Oh!" I replied when it registered. At first, walking around in them felt silly. Later, stuffing was the resolution to fill in gaps. One day, suddenly and without warning, they'd fit just right: not too loose, not too tight!

God, as a great Parent, must know the same secret. So when I first starting serving in ministry, He made sure my shoes were a few sizes too big. I couldn't imagine why until I felt my feet growing. Not only were my steps being ordered, but my shoes were being tailor-made, just like Israel's. I'm His bigger girl, now, preaching in pumps. And He made mine just the right fit... *for the pulpit.*

Epilogue

WHEN I STEPPED out, there was no pattern to follow or people to mock: no one like me. I was a young woman: new to marriage, new to mothering, and new to ministry. I was familiar with a few other female pastors, but we shared no common complexities. If one was a newlywed, she did not have a baby. A few were ordained about the same time I was, but had grown children or marriages with some mileage. Others were single. For the questions I had, I wasn't sure who to ask. God has answered them all as we've walked.

Now, son, to your question that deserves my answer: "Do you like being a pastor?" Most days I actually love it, knowing that through me God shows people the way to Heaven and the abundant road that leads there. Many days I really like it, when entire lives are better because God chooses to use me. We no longer keep record of the countless men, women, and children who have been saved, sanctified, healed, made whole, filled, found, delivered, developed, or became disciples because God "called my phone" to see if I'd relay a message: the gospel.

That good news is both simple and profound: His love is so vast it can cover your then, now, and not yet, and His grace so amazing it can sustain you past time. The message can never change because God will not. A sagacious sister once shared with me that the reason the Lord doesn't change is because He doesn't *need* to. Times change, people change, and situations change. So, our church has only changed *methods* to make room for life.

Son, there are days, few and far between, when I wonder why He dialed my number. Those are days when I have forgotten that these are *His people* and we are *His church*: Descending Dove Christian Center.

THE END

I did not know I would write a book until I started writing. I already wish to try again. Hope you're there. Thanks for being here!

Pastor Angel Wellington's Bio

ANGEL WELLINGTON IS an accomplished teacher, preacher, workshop leader, emcee, and conference speaker. She and her husband pastor Descending Dove Christian Center: an expanding Spirit-infused fellowship in Wilmington, NC, making a powerful permanent impact.

An early interest in television and evangelism led Pastor Angel to study Mass Communications with emphasis in broadcasting. While a sophomore, a last-minute speaking engagement revealed what others had long deduced—a call to communicate *the* message. Responding was daunting since she rejected even the notion of women preachers. Her answer proved costly.

Intense training and mentoring ensued at Faith Deliverance Christian Center under the capable leadership of Dr. Barbara M. Amos. In the office of district overseer, she agreed to assign the Wellingtons to assist a church in North Carolina, where they would later accept the assignment of taking God's people from volatility to productivity.

Kingdom-minded and destiny-determined, she and her husband approach ministry from the vantage point of their personal gifts and abilities, anointed by the Holy Spirit. Pastor Angel is exceptionally creative. She writes, leads worship, acts, directs, decorates, and designs. She is a program coordinator and event planner. With a personal passion to return performing arts back to the Giver, she utilizes all forms of artistic expression to present the Gospel in clear, convicting, and sometimes comedic form. Though she has participated in live recordings, toured with a gospel musical, and hosted radio, the pastoral position has granted a place to bring all those experiences to bear.

Blessed in marriage and motherhood, she and her husband co-labor and are anointed for uncommon couples' ministry. Pastor Angel is resolute about ministry beginning and ending behind closed doors and is pleased to have her family alongside for the ride.

Her out-of-the-box, upbeat, down-to-earth presentation of the good news is undeniably contagious and understandably effective. The message is real, relevant, and relational: not to be dismissed. Pastor Angel Wellington is undoubtedly called to Word ministry, and we are the beneficiaries of her "yes."